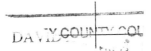

Discovering
Your Old House

Contents

1. Laying foundations 3
2. Essential definitions 6
3. The plan 9
4. Raising the walls 17
5. Raising the roof 35
6. Features 43
7. Developing links 53
8. Aspect 58
9. Libraries 61
10. Pictures and prints, plats and plans 67
11. Doing the deeds 71
12. The naming of houses 77
13. The family home 79
14. Estate houses 80
15. Business 83
16. Quarter sessions 87
17. Local government 89
18. The public records 92
19. Ecclesiastical sources 95
20. Making a survey 99
21. Further housework 102
22. Further reading 104
23. Useful addresses 105
Glossary 106
Index 112

Published in 1997 by Shire Publications Ltd, Cromwell House, Church Street, Princes Risborough, Buckinghamshire HP27 9AA, UK.
Copyright © 1991 by David Iredale and John Barrett. First published as 'This Old House' by David Iredale, 1968; reprinted 1970. Second edition, 'Discovering Your Old House' by David Iredale, 1977; reprinted 1980, 1984, 1987. Third edition, completely rewritten, updated and expanded by David Iredale and John Barrett, 1991; reprinted 1994 and 1997. Number 14 in the Discovering series. ISBN 0 7478 0143 6.

Printed in Great Britain by CIT Printing Services, Press Buildings, Merlins Bridge, Haverfordwest, Pembrokeshire SA61 1XF.

British Library Cataloguing in Publication Data: Iredale, David. Discovering your old house. – 3rd ed. – (Discovering series) I. Title II. Barrett, John III. Series 941.0072. ISBN 0-7478-0143-6.

The cover is by Felix Partridge; the line drawings are by Christine Clerk.

1. Laying foundations

Every house has a tale to tell. This book of hints and encouragements supplies sources and suggestions to enable you as an ordinary householder to begin the discovery of your old house. Discovering your old house requires no more than an enquiring mind, a sensitive eye — and perseverance.

A good way to begin is by seeking information from the people who have been involved with your house in the past. The estate agent who sold you the house may have gathered historical information in order to advertise and value the property. The solicitor who drew up the deeds may have searched on your behalf the ancient papers and parchments which record the property, its owners and occupants, perhaps back to the middle ages. The surveyor who checked the house for signs of damp and dry rot may have noticed some interesting relics of the past such as an inconspicuous fragment of painted medieval wall plaster, or ancient timber now hidden behind the plasterboard.

Neighbours are an invaluable fund of recent history. Elderly local residents in particular are often more than happy to share reminiscences beside a warm fireside, perhaps with a glass of sherry to lubricate the memory and sustain the vocal chords. A notebook and pencil might be useful at this stage, to jot down the names, dates and incidents contained in a garrulous narrative. So that no nuance or anecdote is missed, you might adopt the chief tool of **oral history** and go to interview your neighbours armed with a portable cassette recorder (and a supply of spare tapes and batteries).

It is sometimes possible to contact previous occupants of your house, who may themselves have conducted research into its history. They may be able to show you old photographs and perhaps even original plans for its building or renovation. Some householders assemble affectionate scrapbooks on their homes. If this kind of project appeals, you might take as a model the attractive handwritten account (illustrated with pretty watercolour sketches, maps and plans) compiled by Heywood Sumner before the First World War to record happy memories of his home, Cuckoohill, at South Gorley on the edge of the New Forest (published as *Cuckoohill: the Book of Gorley*, Dent, 1987).

A visit to the local historical or archaeological society (and to the public library) might next prove fruitful — to ask if anyone has made a start on the quest already. Is there anything in print about your old house? The librarian may know of a published book, perhaps the work of a local historian or a former occupant, de-

3

scribing the house. An example of this kind is *Suffolk Oak* by H. J. Fane Edge (Norman Adlard, Ipswich, 1954), which recounts the author's renovation of the delightful timber-framed manor house of Naughton in Suffolk. The librarian may also be able to show you the **statutory list**. This national record of buildings of special architectural or historical interest (listed buildings) includes not only grand and ancient mansions but also quite modest and recent homes (and even inter-war council houses) in both town and country. Here, as an example, is the listing of a manse built for the minister of a Scottish parish in 1854:

CRAGGAN, OLD MANSE, INVERAVON PARISH
CAT: B
Map ref: NJ188 323
Date of Listing: 9.11.87
A & W Reid, Elgin, 1854. 2-storey and attic, S facing symmetrical 3-storey house. Rubble, tooled rubble dressings. Centre door masked by later glazed porch; flanking tripartites with wooden mullions. 2 later piended dormers in outer bays. Centre ground and 1st floor windows in E and W gables; lying-pane glazing throughout, including 2-window rear kitchen wing; 12-pane to dormers. Coped end stacks; graded Banffshire slate roof.
REFERENCES: W Ewing *Annals of the Free Church* ii (1914), p.201. Moray District Record Office, DAW P87.

Take a careful look round your house, making notes and asking questions as you go. Outside the house you might ask: What features look most ancient? What is the house built of — brick, stone, wood? Is it symmetrical? What shape is the roof — is it tiled, thatched or slated? Inside the house you might note changes in the levels of floors or in the thickness of walls — these might be clues to additions and alterations. During redecoration and renovation you might glimpse details usually concealed — by rendering outside or wallpaper inside. Even such a homely study as the history of a house may prove a test of agility, nerve and ingenuity. As you seek to discover every aspect of your home — from foundations to roof — you will spend precarious minutes mounting ladders to examine masonry, pointing and chimney stacks.

If you wish to cast your investigative net wider, it is usually worthwhile taking a look at other houses in the vicinity: houses constructed by the same builder or for the same landlord as your own; houses of similar date; houses similar in style but less altered than yours. This branch of research requires access to other people's homes. Some householders are understandably suspicious of a stranger's interest in their inglenooks and nogging, but an engaging manner and an infectious enthusiasm soon dispel any anxiety.

When discussing your old house with people who do not know it, offer to show them a photograph or, better still, a sketch plan — it is a simple matter to pace out the principal dimensions and to note down any special features of the interior. If you are good at drawing, you might make a pencil or watercolour sketch of those interesting details which sometimes provide a crucial clue to the date of the building, for instance the turned wooden balusters of the stairs or the fancy iron railings (rare survivors of wartime scrap-metal drives) which separate the property from the street.

This preliminary investigation may perhaps inspire you to more ambitious endeavour. The following chapters lead you deeper into the history of your old house. Chapters 2 to 8 show how much can be learned from the building itself: its plan, walls, roof and aspect. Chapters 9 and 10 demonstrate the unexpected variety of information available in pictorial form and in print in the public library. In chapter 11 title deeds are explained. Chapter 12 introduces the broad topic of toponymy (place-names). Chapters 13 to 19 open a door to the mysterious but fascinating subject of archives. And finally, with a glimpse at some possibilities for even deeper research, you are shown how to collect together this welter of information and present it as a polished survey in words, pictures and plans — for your own pleasure and for posterity.

2. Essential definitions

Styles of housing are peculiar to place and time: architectural vernacular is as specific as spoken dialect. **Vernacular style** was dictated by the materials available locally — mellow limestone in the Cotswolds, timber in the south-east, coarse rubble in the highlands. Vernacular style was also determined by local climate, for instance the low rounded hipped roofs of the windy Hebrides. Vernacular houses were designed and built by conservative country craftsmen without academic training — provincial masons and carpenters bound by tradition, sensitive to the qualities of their materials, working to methods and patterns learned through long apprenticeship and practical experience. The antithesis of the vernacular is the polite. **Polite houses** are generally the work of professional architects, executed according to rule and plan. Thus, in architectural terms, the polite house has style rather than charm, order rather than curiosity.

The housing stock of a region, county or town shows epochs of **great rebuilding** — periods of prosperity as merchants, lawyers, yeomen and craftsmen invested the profits of burgeoning trade and fruitful husbandry. Freemen of Kent and Sussex rebuilt their homes as solid stylish wealden houses from the fifteenth century. Glamorgan and Gwent were rebuilt from about 1560. The picture-postcard timber framing of the south-east and the midlands dates from a great rebuilding between 1570 and 1640. English and Welsh highland districts were reconstructed from about 1670; Durham, Northumberland, south and east Scotland, 1720-1815; Ireland, 1780-1845; Scotland beyond the Great Glen, 1780-1890; west Wales, 1850-1914. Rural housing may date from eras of agrarian upheaval, notably from enclosure, clearance and encroftment from about 1750 onwards. Urban housing was renewed as trade and industry expanded, for example Burford in Oxfordshire grew as the wool trade flourished from 1470 to 1690; Pennine Lancashire towns were built as the cotton industry boomed from the 1780s; Dundee was built on hemp, jute and whales after 1850. Following a major catastrophe the housing stock of a town was, perforce, renewed. The town centres of Warwick and Blandford Forum, Dorset, were reconstructed following devastating fires in 1694 and 1731 respectively.

Houses are sometimes classified in geographical terms — as **highland** or **lowland**. In highland Britain (north and west of the Fosse Way, the Roman road running between east Devon and Lincoln via Bath and Leicester) relative poverty deterred householders from instantly adopting every novelty of domestic architecture and

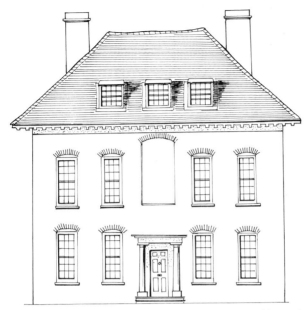

The ideal polite home of about 1690: architect-designed in 'Queen Anne' style for a gentleman in southern England; a symmetrical façade with neo-classical features such as the Doric columns of the doorcase.

accommodation; or perhaps the stone-built houses of the north and west were less readily renovated or renewed than the clay, brick and timber homes of the lowland midlands and south. Both highland and lowland are divided into a kaleidoscope of sub-regions — overlapping traditions of structure, style and materials. Innovation took time to travel across the country. A new architectural feature might take ten years to spread across a county. The direction of movement of innovative features is detectable, in general, from Europe to south and east Britain, from the lowlands to the highlands, and from town to country.

The researcher may conveniently classify houses as great or small. The **great house** was a palace for a prince, landed magnate or industrial plutocrat. The great house provided an example to builders lower down the social scale, who imitated, for instance, the Palladian style of the Queen's House, Greenwich (by Inigo Jones, 1616-35), or the baronial excess of Balmoral (1855). The great house may also fix dates for the first appearance of internal amenities such as central heating (supplementing the open grates of Tullynally, County Westmeath, from 1795), or electric light (installed at Cragside, Northumberland, in 1878 by the armaments tycoon William Armstrong). The **small house** includes the polite residences of the parson and squire as well as the humble homes of ordinary folk — peasant shanty, labourer's cott, yeoman's hall, artisan's terrace. The small-house class also includes speciality housing (gate lodge, bothy, tollhouse, schoolhouse) and those characterful homes which imaginative folk have created in redundant non-domestic buildings (barn, sheepcote, factory, lighthouse, oasthouse, windmill, watermill, warehouse, school and railway station). Deconsecrated churches too are pressed into domestic service, for instance Earl Odda's chapel at Deerhurst, Gloucestershire (dedicated 1056), long lost among the rambling medieval and Tudor additions and encrustations of Abbots Court farmhouse, or Cockley Cley, Norfolk, built as an apsidal church in Saxon times, converted into a dwelling house about 1540, and occupied until 1948.

Quidenham Lodge, Norfolk. This nineteenth-century small house represents an eclectic confection of features attractively composed by a skilled architect for a discerning patron: Flemish gables for front and end elevations; decorative brickwork; vernacularly exterior chimneys flamboyantly suggestive of seventeenth-century style; leaded glass in mullioned windows; and a hint of the medieval in the iron-studded door beneath a round-headed arch. Quidenham was the seat of the Keppel family, followers of William of Orange and, later, Earls of Albemarle. (Photograph: Cadbury Lamb.)

3. The plan

The traditional medieval house was a rectangular **hall** or room in which the whole family ate, slept, lived and died. All the year round a fire of peat or wood burned on an open hearth in the centre of an earthen floor. Poultry roosted among the sooty rafters. The peasant's beasts might be stalled at the lower end of the house, the warmth from their bodies supplementing the heat of the fire, their dung collecting on the floor to manure the fields in the spring. A single doorway served both men and beasts, and so to save her wedding-day petticoats the peasant wife demanded to be carried across the threshold of her matrimonial home. This type of dwelling (*tŷ hir* in Wales) is sometimes referred to as a **longhouse**.

The medieval lord too occupied a hall — a barn-like space of several bays, its stout timber framing supporting a roof of complex carpentry. The family, with friends, relatives, chaplains and servants, shared the communal living-room. Logs blazed in a hearth on the floor, the smoke curling up to a louvre in the roof, blackening the roof beams. In larger timber halls, rows of posts supporting the broad roof formed aisles along the length of the house. The lordly hall was elaborated with a dais at the **upper end**, which raised the gentle family a step above ordinary folk — and above the draughts of the rush-strewn floor. Chilly winds whistled between the opposed doorways.

From the eleventh century onwards a hall might stand at first-floor level above a ground-floor undercroft — a defensive measure supplementing the security of a surrounding moat, palisade and ditch. Such **first-floor halls** were built in both town and country to house, for instance, a laird (Rait, Highland), a placeman (Fishwarden's House, Meare, Somerset), or a city merchant (Jew's House, Lincoln). First-floor halls were still favoured as late as the seventeenth century in Cumbria and the Borders, where they are known as **bastles**. These first-floor blockhouses with their windowless stout stone walls and outside stairs raked by gunloops stand as dour testaments to troubled times.

The medieval hall, open from floor to roof, could be improved by the addition of a two-storeyed **crosswing** at the upper end of the hall. This crosswing contained a private apartment (solar) for the master of the house. The upper storey of the crosswing might protrude (jetty) outwards to overhang the courtyard or street. In East Anglia and the west midlands crosswings projected proud of the hall façade to create a house with an L-shaped ground plan.

Halls with a crosswing at each end (known as **double-ended** houses) were erected from the late fourteenth century onwards,

9

notably in the Weald of Kent and Sussex (and thus referred to as **wealden houses**), but also as far afield as the Welsh Marches and Yorkshire (there built about 1590-1680, often a stone-clad renovation of a timber house). The lower-end crosswing served as a dairy, pantry or buttery with storeroom above; the upper end accommodated living and sleeping rooms. The hall, traditional heart of the house, was recessed, shrinking from prominence between gabled jettied wings. Hall space shrank further with the insertion of a smoke bay or inglenook. An inserted fireplace might obstruct the crosspassage but, to compensate for loss of space, cooking might now safely move indoors, the detached kitchen across the yard being converted into a cottage. Householders in pursuit of privacy and comfort divided their halls horizontally to form upstairs chambers and ground-floor public rooms, and a staircase was now inserted in the heart of the hall.

Jew's House, Lincoln. Designed as a first-floor hall with solar above a vaulted undercroft, this substantial stone house was built for a wealthy (probably not Jewish) merchant around 1160. The Norman date of the original structure is evident in the round-headed masonry arches and the arcaded pattern carved on the voussoirs of the principal doorway. The chimney stack above the entrance arch served the hall fireplace. The original windows consisted of pairs of round-headed openings separated by a central column: a vestige of this Norman fenestration remains in the left upper-floor window. The pantile roof and the Georgian-style sash windows and shop front are recent innovations. (Photograph: David Iredale.)

(Above) Bayleaf, Chiddingstone, Kent. This classic timber-framed wealden house is unusual in having been constructed in two stages, a fact revealed only by very careful dissection of the structure and dendrochronological analysis of the timbers. The hall and service end (right) date from around 1405; the solar end (left) dates from about 1510. The house was subsequently improved with two large chimney stacks, by division of the hall and by addition of a tile-hung wing at the rear. Bayleaf was threatened with inundation by the waters of Bough Beech Reservoir but was saved to be dismantled, removed and restored to original condition at the Weald and Downland Museum, Singleton, West Sussex. The feature cantilevered out from the solar is a convenient garderobe (latrine) — the ordure falling onto a dungheap below ready for spreading on the yeoman's arable furlongs. (Photograph: Cadbury Lamb.)

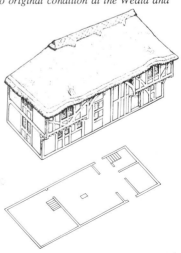

(Right) Double-ended timber-framed (wealden) house with central hall warmed by an open hearth: family apartments at upper end (left); service rooms at lower end (right) beyond the crosspassage.

Valley Farmhouse at Flatford, near East Bergholt, Suffolk. In the timber-framed territory of the Suffolk-Essex border along the valley of the Stour, medieval farmers and merchants waxed rich on the profits of agriculture and woollen manufacture. This prosperity was celebrated in domestic architecture. At Flatford, the late fifteenth-century open hall with hipped and gablet roof and a costly array of close studding was improved with a prominent two-storeyed end. Further elaboration included the stout brick chimney stack, probably inserted when the hall was divided into two storeys. The artist Constable declared of such quintessentially English vistas: 'Those scenes made me a painter.' (Photograph: David Iredale.)

A **two-unit** house comprised a rectangular building divided into two rooms. The front (and normally sole) door opened directly into the chief living-room, a heated hall/kitchen. A smaller, unheated room served for storage, sitting or sleeping. In the **but-and-ben** houses of the north these rooms were known respectively as the but (*be-ūtan*, 'outside') and ben (*be-innan*, 'inside'). The smaller room or ben was also known as the chamber (in the lowlands), the spence (in the north), or the bower (in Cumbria). From about 1650 onwards two-unit buildings were being extended upwards, with chambers created in lofts beneath slates or thatch, lighted, perhaps, by skylights and dormers. Access to upper rooms might be by a dark turnpike (spiral) stair slotted beside the fireplace or set in a projecting turret. The first occupants of upstairs bedrooms were not granted a fireplace and so shivered under their blankets, grateful for whatever warmth rose from the heated rooms below through the floorboards and through the flues within the gable wall. A draughty highland two-unit variant possessed opposed front and back doors opening into a principal living-room with a fireplace on either the gable or rear wall. This type appeared in Scotland and western Ireland from about 1760, northern Wales after 1830.

Central fireplaces beneath conspicuous chimneys were constructed in eastern lowland counties from about 1540. In these compact **axial-stack** houses, back-to-back fireplaces heated the two rooms and dominated the plan: the front door opened into a lobby formed by the fireplace jamb; a turnpike stair was squeezed between fireplace and back wall; the upper floor was divided into two cells by the massive chimney stack. Cramped accommodation was relieved by an unheated parlour set in-line or behind. The awkward entrance was remedied and the elevation dignified by the addition of a front porch standing squarely on the centre line of the axial stack. The plan may have originated at yeoman level in Essex and Kent,

(Below left) Axial-stack house with baffle entry formed by fireplace jamb: back-to-back fireplaces warm the principal rooms; the additional parlour room (right) is unheated.

(Below right) Two-and-a-half unit house, Moray, about 1890: gable-end fireplaces heat the principal rooms; the small central unit was occupied as (ground floor) scullery and (upstairs) bedroom or, later, bathroom.

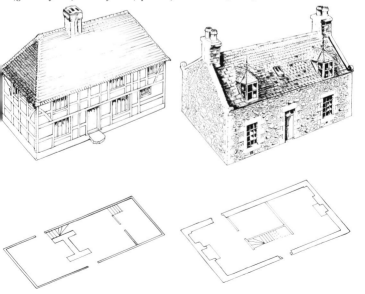

spread to the town hinterlands of Chester and York by 1610, Wales and the rural north of England by 1660, eastern Ireland in the eighteenth century. The style was relatively short-lived — two or three generations in each region.

The **two-and-a-half-unit** house dominated the rural (particularly Scottish) highland housing stock from about 1780. The front door opened into a central room, which might accommodate a box bed or larder. Kitchen and chamber opened to right and left. From about 1840 in newly built two-and-a-half-unit houses the central room (lit by a fanlight over the front door) served as a cramped lobby. Guests hung their mackintoshes over the banisters of the staircase which gave access to attic bedrooms. A scullery or a bedroom (usually unheated) occupied the central cell behind the stairs.

In the **two-plus-one-unit** home of around 1570-1800 an additional room (perhaps a service room with a servant's chamber above) was usually segregated from the main house by a crosspassage and, underlining its lower status, was not (initially) equipped with a fireplace. Though front and back doors normally opened into the crosspassage, eighteenth-century owners frequently added a new porched entrance directly into their main living-room. The Irish two-plus-one of 1780-1850 added to the highland two-unit variant an inner chamber with a small hearth back to back with the kitchen fireplace.

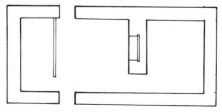

Two-plus-one house in County Clare, about 1845: the inner room (right) is a typical Irish elaboration of a basic two-room tradition at a time of improvement and population growth.

Blackhouse in Benbecula, built around 1790 and improved by the addition of chimneys and enlarged sash windows around 1890: the vernacular housing of island crofting communities.

Polite **double-pile** houses (two rooms deep from front to back) appeared at manor-house level around 1600, and more generally across the south-east by 1650, spreading to the midlands by 1680 and thence into the highland zone. A more vernacular route to double-pile living was by the piecemeal addition of rooms behind a single-pile house — the new outshut covered by a catslide extension to the existing roof. In smart double-piles a front door, centrally placed, opened into a lobby and stairwell. Four ground-floor rooms opened on to this hall: parlour and dining-room (or bedroom) at the front; and two service rooms (variously serving as kitchen, pantry, dairy, library, estate office) at the rear. This centralised circulation heralded a new era of privacy: no longer was it necessary to pass through one room to reach another. This, and a fireplace in every room, made the heavily curtained beds of earlier centuries redundant. Privacy was enhanced and a social separation effected by separate circulation: a narrow stair at the rear of the house enabled servants to pass unseen between their downstairs domain and their cots in the attics.

The double-pile **double-fronted** structure was the basis of more modest houses for the lower orders. A **single-fronted** house (half a double-fronted) comprised an off-centre entrance into a lobby/stairwell giving access to two rooms (front and back) on each floor; basement and attic floors increased accommodation, providing rooms for a lodger or maid. A pantry or scullery was formed beneath the stairs or housed in an outshut extension, in prosperous homes after about 1740, in artisans' dwellings after 1820, in labourers' houses from 1875. A lengthening string of back extensions accommodated such modern amenities as a kitchen, bathroom, wash-house, water (or earth) closet, ashpit and coalshed — innovations which multiplied faster than architects could incorporate them within four walls of the plan. The basic double-pile single-fronted structure could be horizontally subdivided into flats, each of two rooms, or, from about 1790, into pairs of one-up one-down **back-to-back** houses for the factory workers of industrial towns.

15

Stamford, Lincolnshire. Queen Anne style for a gentleman of polite taste: neat ashlar masonry divided at first-floor level by a string course, a symmetrical façade and a hipped tiled roof pierced by a pair of panelled stone chimney stacks. The doorway has a neo-classical doorcase with scrolled pediment. Broadly overhanging eaves (embellished with moulding and shaping of exposed joist-ends) threw rainwater clear of the walls. Servants' attic bedrooms and boxrooms are lighted by a symmetrical array of dormer windows. Windows of the main rooms have been renewed: classic twelve-pane sashes (above) contrast with Oxford-frame variants (below) installed to let more light into ground-floor rooms. (Photograph: Cadbury Lamb.)

4. Raising the walls

Stone

Stone houses were erected at all social levels because, through much of Britain, stone was readily available. Indeed, suitable building stone could be picked up off the ground as rock-strewn land was cleared for agriculture. Stone won from quarries sometimes carries scars which provide a clue to date: marks left by quarrier's wedge, saw and chisel; shot holes to receive a black-powder charge (after about 1780). The condition of stonework too may be a clue to date, provided that allowance is made for accelerated weathering caused by misbedding and acid rain. The reuse of stone from earlier structures was very widespread: rubble for walls was scavenged from stone age cairns and iron age forts, for example. Many homes contain fragments of a despoiled abbey or a demolished castle. The fortunate researcher will identify mason marks — as individual as a signature — cut into the fabric of his home. Record sources may link the master and his mark, supplying a date for the structure and the name of its builder.

In walls of **irregular rubble** the heaviest stones supplied the lower courses. Above this megalithic base a succession of wood, turf and stone walls was raised and demolished, so that the researcher's own house may be but the last in a long line. Hebridean folk extolled the thermal qualities of their rugged cottages. These were of drystone construction, with walls some 1.2 metres (4 feet) thick, comprising a double skin of rubble around an insulating core of peat mould — sufficient against the fiercest gales. Mainland houses were of single-thickness rubble, bedded in clay and packed with small stones. Through-stones penetrating the thickness of the wall bound the structure, sometimes projecting from the wall face as ledges or random protuberances. Dressed stone gave distinction to rubble walls and assisted the builder when turning a quoin and forming a window or door. A wedge-shaped keystone or a relieving arch was essential to lighten loads on door and window lintels in larger houses.

Many dwellings were constructed of smooth squared blocks laid in regular courses (ashlar). Millstone grit, sandstone, limestone and granite were preferred — if only for the public face of the house. From about 1650 onwards smooth stone skins were applied to rough rubble and wooden walls; after 1720 the mask might be fixed to the face with iron cramps.

Water-rounded **cobbles** and ordinary beach pebbles could be used for housebuilding. The stones were bedded in thick layers of clay or mortar and weatherproofed with cement render, limewash

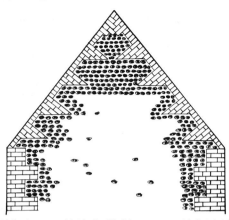

Cobbles laid in courses, thickly bedded in mortar, with bricks to provide a square strong corner (quoin) and, tumbled in, to stabilise the gable.

or (especially in East Anglia) tar. Elongated cobbles were sometimes laid in chevron patterns for decorative effect. Pebble-walled houses, though apparently venerable, are generally no more than two hundred years old.

The **flint** walls of southern and eastern England might, by contrast, date back to the seventeenth century. The white-rinded flint was knapped to expose its pretty black interior: skilled knapping of selected large nodules produced a wall of square glassy blocks. The irregular nodules required generous beddings of mortar and almost invariably were stabilised with lacing courses, quoins, sills, gables and jambs of brick or stone. The felicitous effect of this structural necessity is a dazzling motley of red brick, black flint and pale stone in mansion house and country cottage.

Clay and cob

Clay or cob walls might, if properly built, last for three centuries or more: the earliest surviving (for merchants and yeomen) date from the sixteenth century. The recipe for a durable home required earth or clay trodden to a controlled consistency with careful admixture of stones, sand and chopped straw. The wall was then raised slowly in layers (a division is visible between each) or, with the aid of wood or wattle shuttering, in a single seamless expanse. **Clay-lump** houses were built throughout Britain and Ireland (but notably in Norfolk, Suffolk and Cambridgeshire) from about 1620 to 1800. A clay and straw mix was fashioned into rectangular blocks (45 by 30 by 15 cm; 18 by 12 by 6 inches), which were dried in the sun and built in courses cemented with mud and dung. **Cob**, the Devon and Dorset variety of mud construction, was widely used from 1660 to 1850 in a picturesque vernacular characterised by thick walls, deep-set windows and rounded corners. **Wichert**, a white mixture of earth, clunch and clay in Buckinghamshire, remained fashionable until about 1800. A flimsy hurdling of vertical stakes interwoven with twigs (Old English *ris*) or straw rope was erected to provide reinforcement for a mud-daub wall: examples of this **stake and rice** (and of its close cousin known as **mud and stud**) survive chiefly from the late eighteenth century onwards. **Pisé**, a rammed earth (introduced from France around 1790), was employed for model houses for rural labourers in southern England until about 1860. Earth and clay walls of all kinds were especially susceptible to erosion and thus required a weatherproof skin of limewash or cement render, while stone plinths, tarred lower courses and broadly overhanging eaves offered further protection.

Spreyton, Devon. In the cob houses of south-west England thick mud walls were raised upon firm (often stone) footings and weatherproofed with whitewash or render. Over the years the outward thrust of untied rafters might cause the cob wall to lean, bulge or bow — a condition remedied by the addition of external buttresses. An unassuming open porch, plain casement windows, thick thatch and a late nineteenth-century pump complete an aspect of modest vernacular correctness. (Photograph: John McCann.)

(Top) Brick dimensions are a clue to date: older bricks are thinner than the later standard of 23 by 11 by 8 cm (9 by 4¹/₂ by 3 inches).

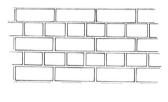

(Centre) English bond: alternating courses of stretchers (bricks laid lengthways) and headers (laid endways).

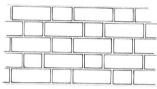

(Bottom) Flemish bond: mixed headers and stretchers in each course.

Brick

Anglo-Saxon and Norman builders were enthusiastic bricklayers, scavenging supplies of thin tile-like brick from Roman ruins. During the thirteenth century, as Roman sites became exhausted, the brickmaker's art was revived and bricks were made for the builders of prestige houses. Commodious brick dwellings for lesser gentry were erected in south-eastern counties from around 1560, Berkshire about 1600, and Nottinghamshire about 1620. The earliest Welsh brickwork dates from the 1560s. At a humbler level, brick first appeared for such limited applications as chimney stacks and gable walls (sixteenth century). The earliest vernacular houses wholly of brick are generally two-storeyed structures dating from the mid seventeenth century. Economic backwardness and conservatism retarded the brick revolution: only one pre-1750 brick house has been recognised in the old county of Caernarfonshire, though brick building was accepted among Irish merchants and farmers by 1720. Brick was used for humble homes in Wales from about 1820 and in the Pennines from the 1870s. But in the highlands of Scotland brick was never widely used: rubble masonry remained the norm until supplanted by cement blocks after 1945.

Bricks measured about 23 cm (9 inches) in length by about 11 cm (4¹/₂ inches) in breadth. The thickness of bricks is a valuable clue to date. Before the middle of the sixteenth century bricks were a slim 5 cm (2 inches), gradually thickening thereafter to about 6

20

Whitley, Cheshire. The Cheshire landscape was enclosed at an early date. Sweeping away medieval peasant communities, landowners installed go-ahead tenants in newly established farms. As the farmers prospered, fine new farmhouses displayed a confidence born of secure tenancies and the profitable promise of the agricultural revolution. The Whitley farmhouse datestone gives 1743 as the date of building — and the occupants' initials. The house, classic in its sash-windowed symmetry, eschews neo-classical fripperies, preferring a simple gabled roof and strong red brick fired on site, made of clay dug from the farmer's own land. (Photograph: David Iredale.)

cm (2½ inches) by 1725 and to 8 cm (3 inches) or more after 1784 (the year a brick tax was introduced). Before about 1660 bricklayers preferred to build one and a half bricks deep (36 cm; 14 inches) but contented themselves with a lighter one-brick (23 cm; 9 inch) or half-brick wall for cheapness. Before about 1620 the uneven textured bricks were laid in a thick (up to 2.5 cm or 1 inch deep) bed of mortar; seventeenth-century joints were a less obtrusive 6-12 mm (¼ to ½ inch). As manufacture improved during the eighteenth century bricks became more consistent in size and texture. With the smooth-faced, sharp-edged Hoffman-kiln brick (1859), bricklayers could work with such precision that the cemented joint between courses might be all but invisible.

Until the end of the seventeenth century bricks varied in colour and texture according to intensity of firing and the chemistry of local clay. Exacting eighteenth-century builders demanded a range of consistent colours and finishes. Intense reds were made in the English midlands about 1720-1820, though not as glaring or shiny red as Accrington or Ruabon bloods of the Queen Anne revival (1865-1910). Silver-grey brick characterised Thames valley pro-

The Crescent, Wisbech, Cambridgeshire. The crescents of the Castle Estate, Wisbech, were begun in 1795, their graceful sweeps outlining the now obliterated Norman fortress. The crescents date from a period of local prosperity based on shipping. The façade of The Crescent is of local red brick, tastefully broken by a white string course and punctuated with neo-classical doorcases with open pediments. The façade is carried above the eaves in a low parapet partly hiding the roof — a style originated in London to comply with local fire regulations and imitated nationwide for aesthetic effect. Each house has a cellar with an iron grating in the pavement. (Photograph: Cadbury Lamb.)

duction of 1740-1810; yellow-brown in London, 1780-1860; yellow through southern England, 1800-50.

A bond is the pattern formed by bricks laid either endwise (headers) or lengthwise (stretchers). Ordinary brickwork before 1640 (and inferior walls later) rarely showed consistent bond. **English bond** (developed from 1560 to 1720) alternated courses of headers and stretchers. A deviant (English garden-wall bond), employing one course of headers with three, five or seven courses of stretchers, was popular in Wales and northern England. **Flemish bond** (fashionable after its introduction at Dutch House, Kew, in 1631) originally alternated headers and stretchers along each course but after 1690 laid three or five stretchers to each header along the course. Experiments with bonds led to more adventurous decorative forays: brick crowsteps (from about 1510); curvaceous Flemish (Dutch) gables (originating in Kent about 1610, politely popular from 1670); cut, rubbed, gauged and moulded bricks for window openings, door cases and relieving arches; string courses to highlight architectural detail. Bricks of contrasting colours and finishes were arranged to emphasise a feature, embellish a façade with diaper, chequerboard and geometrical patterns, or even to spell out a householder's initials and date of occupation.

Wood

Wood supplied the framework of lowland houses until the middle of the seventeenth century and everywhere was indispensable for roof trusses. Manorial woodland was rigorously managed, conscientiously cropped, thinned, felled and replanted to yield a constant supply of timber. For a typical wealden house 330 trees up to 7.6 metres (25 feet) in length and from 15 cm (6 inches) to 46 cm (18 inches) in diameter were needed, with a prodigious quantity of coppice wood for the wattle of the walls.

Oak was the favoured structural timber of the lowlands, though elm and some softwood also had their uses, while the natural curve of the black poplar was valued for cruck blades, notably in Worcestershire and Herefordshire.

The house was prefabricated in the woodland. Sawyers dug their pits in forest clearings, splitting and sawing unseasoned trunks into beams and planks. Carpenters with adze, axe and auger finished and fitted structural members. Each timber was then coded with a notched mark, and the skeleton of the building shipped as a kit for erection in town or village. Exposed timbers were stained red and ochre, weathering naturally to an iron-hard grey finish.

Vertical posts and lateral beams were joined in a variety of mortice and tenon, lap and scarf joints, the mated parts secured with wooden

Lap dovetail joint securing the tiebeam of the roof truss to vertical wallpost and horizontal wallplate.

pegs (trenails). Each joint represents the craftsman's solution to the engineering problems of timbers held in tension or compression, members liable to sagging and side forces. A timber-framed house is thus a lattice of stresses held in a dynamic equilibrium so stable that the whole structure might (in an emergency) be placed on rollers and shifted bodily, in the manner of the fifteenth-century merchant's house at 16 St Edmund Street, Exeter, which was saved from demolition in 1961 by just such an expedient — it now stands as Tudor House, West Street.

Pegged **mortice and tenon joints** were universal in wall framing and so supply few clues to date though a beam tenoned at both ends is likely to be an original. Research is further hampered by the nature of the mortice and tenon, whose construction is fully visible only when the joint is dismantled, though pegs and pegholes provide useful clues.

Lap joints trenched crossing timbers into one another for strength and neatness. A dovetail prevented a beam-end under tension from pulling free. At the wallhead where wallplate, rafter, tiebeam and post met in four planes a lap-dovetail and tenon assembly mated the members.

Scarf joints secured beams in-line. Beam-ends were halved and notched with mirror-image cutaways, then drilled and secured with pegs and wedges. Simple edge-halved pegged scarfs are known from Saxon times. Fifteenth-century carpenters rotated the scarf through 90 degrees though this innovative face-halved scarf (with bladed rather than bridled abutments) was not widespread until the sixteenth century. By this date, however, pure carpentry had become infected with ironmongery — screws, nails, bolts, studs and girders.

A **cruck-framed** house employed pairs of inclined timbers (blades) joined at the apex to serve as both a main roof truss (carrying longitudinal roof purlins) and an internal skeleton for non-structural outer walls. Blades were joined into a rigid A-frame by tiebeam or collar. The frames, linked by longitudinal purlins, divided the structure into bays, each about 2.4 to 4.9 metres (8 to 16 feet) long. Full crucks, rising from wall foot to roof ridge, have been identified as early as 1275, though surviving full crucks are mostly of the fifteenth and sixteenth centuries. Base crucks were

(Left) Complex scarf joint with tongue-and-groove elaborations and with undercut (under-squinted) surfaces for additional strength; secured by pegs at both face and edge, and held tight by a wedge (transverse key).

(Right) Scarf joint: face-halved with four edge pegs; elaborated with extensions (blades) to each member, preventing lateral movement.

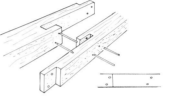

(Left) Complex scarf joint, the timbers shaped to meet at an acute angle (splayed), with undercut (under-squinted) surfaces for additional strength, held tight by a wedge (transverse key), and secured by four face pegs — a joint to resist sagging, hogging and twisting forces

(Right) Simple edge-halved scarf joint with square abutments secured by two face pegs.

Two-bay cruck frame: the longitudinal members (purlins) supported roof rafters (not shown); walls were raised, free-standing, outside the crucks and bore little of the weight of the roof.

truncated below their potential apex and joined at the top by a stout horizontal beam. Raised, middle and upper crucks were planted on the firm footing of an outside wall, springing from the wallhead or from partway up the wall, creating airy loft spaces in cob and stone-walled houses as two-storey living became usual during the seventeenth century.

In a **post and truss** or **box-framed** house, vertical main posts supported the longitudinal member (wallplate) at the wallhead. Opposing main posts were joined by a transverse tiebeam, from which sprang a principal roof truss.

In both crucks and box-frames, load-bearing timbers and intermediate studs outlined a pattern of panels. In **large framing** the panels were some 1.8 metres (6 feet) square. Large frames benefited from diagonal bracing: arch bracing in the midlands, tension bracing in the south-east. Braces multiplied into parallel, herringbone and St Andrew's cross patterns. In **close studding** vertical members divided a façade into narrow panels (of storey height or interrupted by a middle rail). Diagonal braces are usually present,

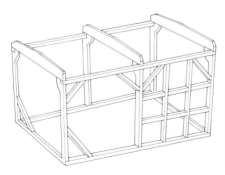

Two-bay box frame: the principal posts and longitudinal wallplate supported roof trusses and rafters; wall panels were infilled with wattle and daub or brick.

though concealed. Close studding was installed (perhaps only on the street front) chiefly for display; sometimes the studs were not even pegged into the structural frame. **Small framing** (also known as square framing), characterised by panels some 60-90 cm (2-3 feet) square (two or three panels to each storey), percolated down the social scale by the end of the seventeenth century. **Ornamental framing** from the late sixteenth century marked the ostentatious pinnacle of timber-frame construction. From Kent to Yorkshire neat small panels with curving braces chequered the façades of prosperous homes, most famously in the cusped and quatrefoil patterning of Cheshire and Lancashire.

(Above) Decorative small framing: structural (and non-structural) timbers arranged and shaped to form fashionable cusped, quatrefoil and herringbone patterns and panels.

(Below) Close studding: vertical timbers (studs) — some load-bearing, some simply decorative — arranged in close-set ranks as a form of conspicuous display, notably in eastern England.

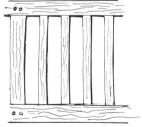

(Left) Vernacularly off-centre porch with decorative small framing at 20 High Street, Castle Donington, Leicestershire, dated 1636.

Bromyard, Herefordshire: 4 and 6 The Square. The site of this timber-framed merchant's house has been occupied since the planned town was established in the twelfth century. The cellar (note the grating in the pavement) is claimed, tentatively, as Norman. The house and shop as presently seen are modelled around a late fifteenth-century core (officially listed as 'eighteenth-century or earlier'). The ornamental framing is typical of the later sixteenth century. The attic storey was created perhaps in the course of eighteenth-century renovations, which also included the lowering of the roof pitch and the substitution of slates for thatch. The sixteen-pane sashes are also eighteenth-century innovations. The shop door has moved several times, though two of the Regency-style bay windows are original. The historian of houses, like the collector of antiques, soon learns to distinguish the real from the reproduction, and the honestly restored from the deliberately faked. (Photograph: Cadbury Lamb.)

Lavenham, Suffolk. Though perhaps small by modern standards, this range of single-pile timber-framed building represents the upmarket housing of the wealthy businessmen of Suffolk during the boom years of the wool trade around 1500. The style of the dwelling proclaims the status of the occupant, who, shunning old-fashioned open-hall living, demanded upstairs chambers above downstairs parlours and business premises. The adoption of a two-storey lifestyle is announced in a prominent jetty and exposed upper-floor joist ends. Close studding of expensive oak timbers, typical of East Anglia — and far in excess of structural requirements — further proclaims the prosperity of the householder. The steep roof pitch may suggest an original thatch covering, though on this house the hand-made local clay tiles may be an original feature. The chimney is set to one side of the ridge and may be a later insertion. The gable-end stair may incorporate a medieval upstairs privy. (Photograph: Cadbury Lamb.)

Jettied upper storeys were fashionable from about 1350 to 1620. An attractive feature whose structural function has been much debated, they are best explained as status symbols. Until about 1450 the projecting joists of overhanging storeys were protected (and emphasised) by a fascia board. From the late fifteenth century the bones of the building were prominently displayed: carved dragon beams, posts and brackets (where jetties met at right angles), bressumers and joist ends. During the seventeenth century less exuberant tastes prevailed, and outside timbers were smoothed and understated.

Elm Hill, Norwich. The Monastery and The Coffee House complete the vista of Elm Hill, 'one of the finest medieval streets in Europe', which was saved and restored by the Norwich Society and the Civic Trust. These houses exhibit the usual medieval urban façade of several jettied storeys, carved dragon posts and exposed joisting. Features resulting from subsequent renovation include sash windows, pantiled roofs and modern pastel colour. These two late medieval merchants' houses have undergone several changes of use. The seventeenth-century Monastery (left) is named from its occupation in 1864 by the Anglo-Catholic brotherhood of the Reverend J. L. Lyne (Father Ignatius). The Coffee House (right), a fifteenth-century structure, was for a time a public house (the King's Head, changed to the Briton's Arms in 1804) and has also accommodated the headquarters of the Norfolk Wherry Society and a buffet restaurant. (Photograph: David Iredale.)

Infilling and cladding

The timber skeleton was infilled with non-structural panels. Pointed staves were sprung into grooves chiselled into the edges of the timbers. Withies of hazel and ash or laths of beech and oak were woven between the staves and sealed with a daub of clay and dung bound with straw or hair. The **wattle and daub** panels were finished with a weatherproofing of lime plaster, perhaps tinted from a limited range of earth colours. (The dazzling magpie livery is a latter-day affectation achieved by copious application of nineteenth-century black preservative and twentieth-century brilliant white.)

Bricks infilled timber frames from the fifteenth century at merchant and gentry level, but rarely at vernacular level before 1650. **Brick nogging** might replace dilapidated wattle and daub on older houses, though numerous lowland houses were nogged when first built, the slim bricks laid in decorative herringbone patterns.

Weatherboarding was applied to East Anglian houses from the sixteenth century onwards. Oak or elm planks were pegged (later, deals were nailed) to the studs and beams of the timber frame. Imported softwood (painted white or tarred black) was popular from 1790 as clapboarding for slightly built timber-framed housing in south-eastern counties.

Tile hanging may have originated in Kent around 1690. Plain clay tiles (hung by peg or nail) and lugged tiles (hung on laths)

(Below left) Wattle and daub panel, cut away to show vertical staves interwoven with hazel withies and coated with mud, dung and plaster.

(Below right) Brick nogging: bricks to infill a timber frame, here laid in decorative herringbone pattern between close-set studs.

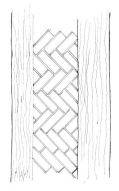

Lamb Cottage, Church Street, Chiswick, London. This house was once a public house, the Lamb Tap, and village pubs always repay investigation. Beneath the weatherboard skin and Georgian-style windows is a singular structure with an intriguing jetty. The bay window and brick-built bar extension are closely documented in local building control and licensing magistrates' records and in planning files. Title deeds once held by the brewer should now have been handed over to the present owner or lodged with his solicitor or building society. (Photograph: Cadbury Lamb.)

were specially favoured as cladding for the poorer wooden housing of the south-east between 1780 and 1850. Occasionally a tile-hung timber upper storey was added to a brick ground floor, perhaps to save weight on foundations or the expense of brick tax (1784-1850). **Mathematical tiles** (also known as mechanical or brick tiles) sumptuously passed for brick while avoiding the tax. These fake bricks were tile-hung usually only on the street façade — often to mask a rickety timber frame or an offensively vernacular complexion of flint, cobble or pebble. Mortar pointing with voussoirs, sills, quoins and doorcases of painted stone-look wood completed the illusion — to the discomfiture of more than one cursory researcher.

A complete skin of weatherproof plaster could be used to seal potential leaks between panels and studs, completely concealing tell-tale timbering from the researcher's view. The plaster was applied to wooden laths nailed across the face of the house. From the late sixteenth century the wet plaster might be combed into low-relief patterns of chevron, basketweave, cable and fan. By about 1670 this decorative **pargeting** (especially in East Anglia) was worked into exuberant high-relief designs — hatchments, fleurs-de-lis and grotesque masks perhaps highlighted with colour. Such decorative excess fell from favour in the eighteenth century and, while a few genuine examples were preserved as antiquarian curiosities, pargeting visible today is generally the work of restorers and revivalists.

An applied **stucco** skin could also protect an unsound structure and conceal a multitude of impolite sins. A full coat of cement **harling** or roughcast (lime mixed with gravel) improved the rubbly complexion of highland walls. Three-quarter harling sealed joints in clay-bonded rubble while leaving some flat stone surfaces exposed to shed water. Liardet's cement (1773), receptive of a fine polish, Parker's Roman cement (1796) and Aspdin's Portland cement (1824) transformed drab stock brick, timber or rubble into polite ashlar, with joints, quoins and pilasters drawn with a mason's trowel on the wet cosmetic. From 1900 onwards a rash of **pebbledash** (dry dash) infected the housing stock — a water-shedding coating and a finish which might individuate or standardise the bricks and blocks of suburbia.

Bishop Bonner's Cottage, East Dereham, Norfolk. This late medieval house originally comprised a hall with a jettied end, later divided into two storeys with the addition of brick chimneys. It is associated with Edmund Bonner, who became a bishop and under Mary I a persecutor of Protestants. Medieval folk enjoyed colour and decoration on the inside and the outside of their homes. Here, relief patterns in plaster (pargeting) of coiling foliage picked out in bright paint are reminiscent of the opulent borders of illuminated manuscripts. The fishscale tile-hanging on the gable and the whimsical dormer are uncharacteristic modernities. (Photograph: David Iredale.)

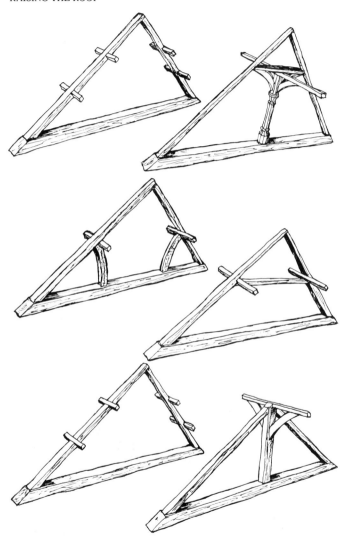

Roof trusses (clockwise from top left): butt purlin; crown post; clasped purlin; king post; through purlin; queen post.

5. Raising the roof

The shape, span and construction of a roof were influenced by a variety of factors: its date; the personal preference of the owner or designer; the plan of the house; the choice of material for the walls; the length and quality of timber available for the roof; and the type of weatherproofing available for the roof covering. From a tangle of timbers in the roofspace the researcher can unravel a hidden history.

The simplest roof was composed of paired rafters — halved, jointed and pegged at the apex, perhaps triangulated at the foot, usually reinforced by a horizontal collar into an A-shaped frame, and perhaps strengthened further by criss-cross scissor braces or parallel rafters. The rafters, collars and braces of a **rafter single roof** might serve as studding for a timber or plaster ceiling.

A second class of roof included longitudinal members (side purlin, collar purlin or ridge) to stiffen the structure. In the simplest of these the purlins or ridge linked an unpunctuated rank of identical common rafters. A classic roof style incorporating longitudinal stiffening (installed in houses from the later thirteenth century) consisted of a **crown post** rising from a tiebeam to support a longitudinal collar purlin (crown plate) connecting the collars of the rafters. Crown post, collar and purlin were linked by arching struts and brackets. The crown post itself, a polygonal shaft some 15 cm (6 inches) in diameter and 1.8 metres (6 feet) in height, with moulded base and capital, and sometimes chamfered, was adopted as a badge of rank. Crown posts descended from lordly halls to yeomen's homes to become a general lowland style during the fifteenth century, superseded thereafter by paired purlins clasped between collar or strut and principal rafters (clasped purlin).

For timber-framed houses, particularly in the north of England from about 1450 onwards, the principal roof truss comprised a vertical **king post** rising from tiebeam to apex to support a longitudinal ridge member. The king post, a stout 20 cm (8 inches) square by 1.8 metres (6 feet) long, added an austere strength to heavy stone-tiled roofs battered by northern gales. During the sixteenth century collars rose and king posts shrank into short functional struts that did not obstruct attic chambers.

Side purlins carrying the ranks of common rafters were supported by the blades of the main roof trusses (principal rafters). In a butt-purlin roof (a common form during the period 1580-1760) the side purlins either passed through or were butted against (and tenoned into) the principal rafters. In a through-purlin roof (usually associated with crucks and king posts) the purlins rested on, or were trenched into, the backs of cruck blades and principal rafters.

Thatch was a usual roofing material until the mid nineteenth century. Prosperous lowland homes were thatched with a dense layer of selected reed or straw, secured to laths laid across the rafters. The hazel sways which held the thatch in place were arranged in patterns varying from region to region and from thatcher to thatcher. From the 1870s individual craftsmen added playful signatures to their work, perhaps in the form of a straw-sculpted peacock or a squirrel to perch upon the ridge. On upland roofs thin turves rested on a mesh of cords laced between the rafters; on to this bed was laid a tousled mat of barley straw, bracken and heather, secured against the plucking of rooks and westerlies by weighted straw ropes and (from the eighteenth century onwards) by ragged redundant fishing nets. Irish and Scottish roofs were stripped every two or three years and the soot-heavy thatch composted on

Lower Tor Farm, Widecombe-in-the-Moor, Devon. Lower Tor was constructed as a substantial thatched granite longhouse during the sixteenth century. A single wide through-passage entrance originally gave access to the house (left) and the byre (right). The house end consisted of two rooms, both heated, with attic chambers reached by a turnpike stair. During the eighteenth century the house was dignified with a porch with moulded arched entrance (inscribed 'IT 1707') and the byre was reconstructed with its own through-passage entrance. The final separation of people from animals occurred later when the cattle were evicted and the byre-end absorbed into the house, ultimately to serve as a kitchen. (Photograph: David Iredale.)

County Clare, Ireland. The Irish rural vernacular house of the age of agricultural improvement (from 1780 onwards) comprised a comfortable two-plus-one dwelling built by local craftsmen using local materials. The walls are of clay-bonded rubble upon which frequent and generous applications of whitewash build up to form a thick waterproof skin. The low-pitched roof is covered with a plain straw thatch suitable to the wet and windy climate of a western county. Sometimes all three rooms were supplied with a fireplace, and a windowless loft under the thatch might serve as a bedroom for the children. (Photograph: John Barrett.)

dungheaps or spread fresh to manure fields and gardens. Thatched roofs were generally set at a steep angle (50-60 degrees) with a broad overhang to throw rain clear of the wall. Hebridean roofs were rather lower-pitched and designed to run water from the thatch on to the turf-covered wallhead, thence percolating through the peaty core of the wall. Throughout Britain thatch has been replaced, for example by tile, slate or corrugated iron, but steep pitches survive to indicate a roof formerly thatched.

Broad **stone flags** and trim **stone tiles** were hung by oaken pegs to roofs wherever suitable limestones, sandstones and schists were locally available: low-pitched (30 degrees) for the megalithic flags of Orkney and Caithness, steeper (50 degrees) for the trim tiles of the Cotswolds. Steeper pitches may be indicators of a stone roof originally thatched. Stone tiles were usually graded — largest at the eaves, smallest at the ridge — while individually dressed tiles swept the roof around the intricate shapes of dormers and tower-house turrets and neatly finished the angle of a hip.

In the Lake District, Wales, the Isle of Man, Leicestershire and western Scotland **slate** was quarried for roofing. The green and grey roofs of Cumbria and Scotland present a pleasantly ragged texture from the raw edges and irregular width of individual slates. Slate was restricted to the narrow hinterland of the quarry until the transport revolution (1760-1880) permitted its shipment across the country from quarry to the cities. Then thin purple Welsh slate, precisely cut to standard sizes, spread across Britain's roofs, replacing local thatch, slab, tile and flag. The grey monotony of this roofscape might, however, be enlivened with decorative designs, for instance fish-scale slates to cap a conical mock-baronial turret. Slated roofs may be pitched as low as 30 degrees, though they are usually steeper for aesthetic reasons. On the other hand the steep pitches of thatched roofs were lowered to receive a heavy covering of slates, perhaps as part of an extensive renovation involving raising

Church Street, Ribchester, Lancashire. Nineteenth-century prosperity in Ribchester was based on cotton manufacture. Mill workers lived in houses of roughly hewn coursed stone (with datestones of the 1790s). Handloom weavers set up their looms in backyard sheds and converted attics. These terraced houses offered two main rooms on each floor and a backyard reached through a tunnel-like passage. The owners of these listed buildings have installed new windows in prominent stone surrounds. The house in the centre has period-reproduction leaded glass and antique-style door furniture. The house furthest right retains workshop-attic windows but received genteel two-light refenestration around 1910. (Photograph: Cadbury Lamb.)

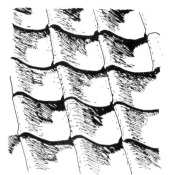

Terracotta pantiles, each tile over-lapped by the tile to the right and the tile above. They were introduced into eastern counties from about 1630.

the walls to create an attic floor lighted by dormers. Slating was double-lapped in diminishing courses, fixed with iron nails to battens and planks (sarking) nailed across the rafters.

Plain rust-brown **tiles** of fired clay appeared on London roofs during the twelfth century, the fashion spreading across the south-eastern counties, though remaining a relative rarity elsewhere before about 1580. From the 1620s onwards Dutch manufacturers began to flood the British market with mass-produced tiles. Tile size was fixed by regulations of 1477 and 1725 at $10^1/2$ inches by $6^1/4$ inches by $5/8$ inch (267 by 159 by 16 mm), though in practice size varied significantly between batches and manufactories. Tiled roofs are generally steep-pitched. The tiles were fixed to laths by means of a wooden peg, iron nail or moulded lug. The curved profile and variety in colour and finish of hand-made tiles gave roofs a rippling texture, in contrast to the flatter finish of the machine-made nineteenth-century product.

After 1630 imported Dutch **pantiles** appeared on the roofs of eastern England. From 1700 onwards home-produced pantiles spread to Yorkshire and Scotland. However, except for an eccentric tradition in Somerset and Wiltshire, pantiles did not become popular in the western counties. The pantile (usually about 343 by 241 by 13 mm; $13^1/2$ inches by $9^1/2$ inches by $1/2$ inch) was formed from a rectangular slab of clay bent into an S-shape. Pantile roofs are generally low-pitched, with tiles single-lapped. Lateral overlays sealed the side joints and, to prevent penetration by wind, rain and snow, gaps were plugged with a mixture of clay bound with hair (torching).

Pitched roofs were gabled or hipped according to local taste, tradition and climate. A simple **gable** was the norm for highlander and lowlander. A **double-gable** roof covered earlier double-pile houses, giving an M-shaped elevation and continual trouble from damp ceilings beneath valley gutters clogged by birds' nests and rotting leaves. The **hipped and gablet** roofs of wealden houses rose as lofty statements of status above the gabled roofs of lesser lowland folk. On Hebridean houses and Irish cabins low rounded

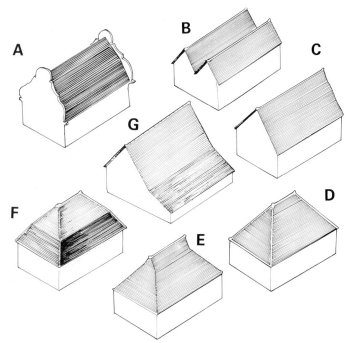

Types of roof: A, pitched roof with Flemish gables; B, M-shaped gables for a double-pile house; C, standard pitched roof; D, hipped roof; E, hipped and gabled roof; F, mansard roof; G, catslide roof over outshut.

hips resisted the western gales and economised on precious structural timber collected as driftwood on the shore or reused through several generations. A half hip offered enlarged loft space lighted by a gable-end window, particularly in polite cottaging. Demand for usable attic rooms was answered by continental architects, notably François Mansart (1598-1666), who gave his name to the mansard roof, constructed with a double slope. The **mansard** appeared on large houses during the late seventeenth century, its broad garrets accommodating the regiment of staff who serviced the Georgian home.

Roof details are peculiar to place and time. Ridges were capped with plain functional clay tiles or dressed stone, though nineteenth-century roofs sported a rash of orange and cream terracotta, moulded crests, iron cressets and Gothick finials. At the eaves the architect

40

might add a moulded wooden cornice (perhaps serving as a gutter) or a parapet (concealing a gutter). The broadly overhanging eaves of the Renaissance house (1660 onwards) were developed with eye-catching moulding, treated with brilliant white-lead paint. At cottage eaves a plain overhang threw rainwater clear of the walls on to the ground below. Lead gutterings became widespread from the eighteenth century with downpipes initially square in section — but beware the false clue of an antiquarian's misdated rainwater head. Cast iron replaced lead in the nineteenth century.

Where local taste required a projecting verge, the roof was finished with a **bargeboard**. This protective planking offered a surface for decoration: cusping and carved spandrels (1420-1530); vine leaves, dangling pendants and classical motifs (1590-1640); Tyrolean fretting and scalloping (1860-1910). Where the roof did not sail across the gable wall the wallhead was weatherproofed with a plain stone **skew**. The joint between skew and wallhead was stabilised with a **skewput**. Plain vernacular skewputs were elaborated from the eighteenth century in a flourish of scrolls and ogee mouldings. **Crow-stepped gables**, a flight of dressed blocks, from the early sixteenth century imparted a fashionably craggy ambience to houses in east Britain, from the lairdly towers of the highlands to the merchant homes of East Anglia. An arched puttstone (inscribed with a date of construction) finished the flight at the wallhead. From about 1670 to 1720 the curvaceous shaped gable marked Dutch influence in eastern counties.

Details of houses in Forres, Moray, Grampian. (Left) The skewput, which finished the slope of a stone gable at the wallhead, offered a suitable surface for carved decoration; this design is dated, scrolled and cabled. (Right) An arching puttstone finishes this traditional crow-stepped gable.

Braco's House, Elgin, Moray, Grampian. This merchant's house of harled rubble with graded stone-tile roof shows a blend of vernacular features (such as crow-stepped gables and dormer windows) with polite architecture (a balanced façade with twelve-pane sash windows). The High Street of the burgh of Elgin was once lined with these elegant dwellings, which represent a 'great rebuilding' of the town during the prosperous generation around 1700. The arcaded ground-floor piazzas (disapproved of by Dr Johnson in 1773) encroached forward of the medieval building line to provide a covered walkway for pedestrians but were subsequently incorporated into the merchants' shops and ultimately fitted with plate-glass display windows. Carved on the triangular panels above the dormers of this property are the initials 'ID' with a thistle motif (for John Duncan) and 'MI' with fleur-de-lis (for Margaret Innes, Duncan's wife) and the date 1694. The building later served as the banking house of William Duff, laird of Dipple and Braco, ancestor of the Earls of Fife. (Photograph: John Barrett.)

6. Features

Floor

The medieval floor was of earth, bound with bullock's blood, hard-packed by use, strewn with rushes and sweet herbs. Highland halls might be paved with flagstones — a chilly flooring which (supplemented by brick, quarry tile or cement) remained standard for labourers' houses and the service domain until the twentieth century. Unbarked split logs, laid on the damp earth, supplied sufficient, if primitive, joisting for plank floors, into the eighteenth century, though **joists** let into the wall with free circulation of air below proved less prone to rot. Until the sixteenth century joists were laid flat rather than on edge, a practice which allowed builders to employ crooked timbers, split and sawn, then squared to yield a pair of mirror-image members. To the heart faces of these curving supports were pegged the floorboards.

For flooring upper rooms, yeomen and merchants required sturdy parallel beams with recessed shoulders to receive broad alternating planks of pit-sawn oak. During the sixteenth century builders gradually adopted a smaller (13 by 10 cm; 5 by 4 inch) joist laid on its narrow edge as the basis of fully framed floors. Dating guides to **floor framing** include the bare-faced soffit tenon (after 1350); the central tenon with housed soffit shoulder (1450); the soffit tenon with diminished haunch and mortice, with diminishing sunken butment cheek (1550). Joists spanned the house, supported at the ends on a horizontal **girding beam** incorporated into the wall frame. Long spans were managed by tenoning joists into a bridging beam. Oak floorboards were traditionally pegged (later, deals were nailed) at right angles to the joists. Bridging beams above ground-floor rooms might be chamfered and moulded or, in high-quality building, multiplied into a coffered ceiling of rectangular panels, each perhaps painted with a monogram, hatchment or heraldic device. Thin 15 by 5 cm (6 by 2 inch) softwood joists and neat narrow elm, fir and pine planks became standard during the eighteenth century.

Internal walls

While medieval woodwork remained fashionable, the studs and beams of the timber frame and **plank and muntin** partitioning were exposed indoors. From the sixteenth century oak wainscoting might be installed to cover internal walls in rectangular panels of **linenfold** carving. From 1580 wainscots were formed of small squarish 60 cm high (2 foot) recessed panels. After 1650 softwood wainscoting consisted of large upper and small lower panels with recessed framing and bolection mouldings. Pine panelling of narrow

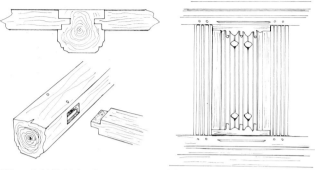

(Above left) Bridging beam to support joists spanning a broad upper floor; the timbers join in a central tenon joint with housed soffit shoulder, secured by a single face peg.

(Above right) Linenfold panelling: the decorative finish for wainscoting of principal rooms in a sixteenth- or seventeenth-century house (revived in the nineteenth century).

(Below) Smoke bay formed of timber framing; smoke-blackened timbers in the roofspace may betray the former existence of a smoke bay.

(7.5-15 cm; 3-6 inch) planks was favoured from 1780 onwards, dividing the interiors of rubble-walled homes into snug wooden boxes.

The plastered walls of medieval interiors might be decorated with paint, either fresco or tempera, depicting floral designs, saints and moral lessons. Domestic decoration sustained this artistic genre long after its erasure from the parish church by the righteous whitewash of puritanism.

During the sixteenth century pargeters set to work indoors, moulding cornices, hatchments, monograms and Renaissance swags on the ceilings of the gentry. Pargeted patterns moderated under the restraining influence of academic classicism during the

Inglenook fireplace at Arnolds Farm, Lambourne, Essex, dating from around 1550 fitted with comfortable benches at the fireside and shelves behind, where food might be kept warm.

eighteenth century, except in the grandest houses, where every detail sprang in gilded relief from cool blue or green and rich red backgrounds. Nineteenth-century rooms were finished with a plaster cornice: deeply sculpted in master bedroom and drawing-room; simple by-the-yard mouldings for the nursery. At the centre of the ceiling an extravagant plaster rose concealed the flue which extracted fumes from a pendant gasolier.

Hearths and chimneys

A hearth on the floor warmed rich and poor alike throughout the middle ages. Smoke from an open hearth curled to the roof ridge, blackening beams and rafters before filtering out through central louvre or open gablet. Exceptionally in stone-built halls from the twelfth century onwards the fire was confined beneath a masonry chimney. Sixteenth-century householders reassessed their heating requirements: the sulphurous fumes of the new fangled seacoal fires offended nostrils accustomed to wood or peat smoke; and the fashion for upstairs chambers and ceiled living-rooms made open hearths impracticable. The hearth was relocated to a **smoke bay**, set beneath a **smoke hood** (a primitive timber-framed chimney fireproofed with thick daubings of clay and plaster), or confined beneath a **chimney stack**. Stone or brick stacks were slotted into an existing smoke bay or screens passage, or buttressed against an outside wall. Cavernous **inglenook** fireplaces created a snug room within a room. High temperatures might shatter brick and stone, so gentlemen purchased iron **firebacks** (from about 1620), protecting hearth backs with a flourish of heraldic cast iron.

The brick revolution of the sixteenth century offered new opportunities for display as chimneys rose in joyous follies of spiral, fluted and chevron brickwork dominating the roofscape. During the seventeenth century rectangular pairs, rows or clusters of stacks were linked at the top with oversailing brickwork. The formal style of the eighteenth century arranged chimney stacks into neat slabs unified by a moulded coping. A recessed clay pot protected the stack from extremes of temperature, while twisting flues within the thickness of the walls conducted smoke from grates throughout the house. During the nineteenth century flues were lined throughout their tortuous length with earthenware pipe, and the stack sprouted a battery of terracotta pots and whirling,

(Above) Brick chimneys at Brent Eleigh, Suffolk, about 1620, with fancy brickwork built in oversailing courses.

dog-legged, galvanised or rusty patent chimney cans.

For coal fires an iron basket was fitted into older hearths. The more efficient **register grate** (around 1750), framed by an arch of decorative cast iron, acquired back and side plates extending into the flue, with a door to close off the chimney and

(Above) Panelled ashlar chimney stack of about 1820, with terracotta chimney pots of about 1890.

(Right) 'Lanco' unitary kitchen range by Ellkay and Company, 1912.

regulate draughts. Hobs and trivets facilitated cooking. The slow combustion grate incorporated a firebrick lining (1850) and an adjustable front canopy (1880). Hot-water central heating was introduced in the 1830s, though inefficient Victorian boilers, pipes and radiators required supplementing with open fires. The kitchen **range** with combined iron oven and grate was introduced around 1770. Pots hung from iron chains over the open grate. Water boilers were added by 1815. In the closed range (1802) the grate was covered by a hotplate: the classic unitary 'Leamington kitchener' of the 1820s consisted of two ovens (baking, roasting) with water boiler behind. In 1815 the freestanding portable range was patented, the ancestor of the coke-burning Aga (1924).

Stairs

By means of a simple ladder or a recessed companionway, the lord of the manor ascended from hall to solar, the peasant clambered from firehouse to loft. The castle-owning class enjoyed the convenience of stone **spiral stairways** coiling up dark shafts within the thickness of their rubble walls. Turnpike stairs were installed in the two-storeyed homes of the sixteenth century — a spiral of keyhole-shaped stones or timbers meeting in a central newel. Generally, such stairways were slotted in where the plan permitted (perhaps cramped between fireplace jamb and outer wall), though for display stone stair turrets were projected from the façades of highland homes, topped by a corbelled chamber or a jaunty conical cap. A variation of this theme comprised a staircase of straight flights and right-angle turns rising around a square core. During the seventeenth century framed wooden **newel** staircases appeared, rising between floors in right-angle flights with balusters of fretted slats and carved newels. The more compact **dog-leg** version involved a 180 degree turn. Both types included a half landing. Eighteenth-century balusters were turned and twisted; and stairways were lighted with stained, etched and painted glass windows.

Doors

The peasant husbandman secured his few possessions behind a rude plank door fastened with a wooden latch or drawbar. The more substantial of medieval doors have survived: stout iron-studded oak planks hung on iron strap-hinges or on iron pins leaded into masonry door frames. A tower-house entrance invoked a double line of defence: a door to keep out the weather and a gate (**yett**) of interlaced iron to keep out raiders and rival chiefs. Medieval doorways (until around 1560) were shaped to the Gothic taste of the time — with pointed, ogee, three or four-centred arch —

Neo-classical doorcase for a first-rate house in Georgian Dublin: the fanlight (above) lights the hallway within while a lamp placed in the projecting glazed central box illuminated the doorstep.

though usually lower and narrower than convenient for the modern visitor. During the later seventeenth century neo-classical tastes required rectangular **framed doors** of three panels (six panels 1740-1810, four panels thereafter), while the doorcase gathered voussoirs, pediments, cornices, brackets, pilasters and columns in a catholic range of orders. The dim lobby behind the door was lit by a fanlight embellished with decorative tracery. From around 1770 a growing array of iron and brass furniture cluttered door and doorstep: link snuffer, name plate, boot scraper, door handle, bell-pull, lock plate. Statutory house numbering dates in London from 1767, in Scotland from 1833, and in the rest of England, Ireland and Wales from 1847. Letter boxes appeared in ordinary front doors as the Post Office achieved its target of delivery to every house by the time of Queen Victoria's Diamond Jubilee (1897).

Windows

Windows were shaped to suit the householder's pocket and taste, and also the proportions of the room — long and low for parlour and solar, wide and tall for open hall, projecting **oriels** (after 1450) for an upper chamber. Windows were barred with moulded stone or square-cut wooden mullions. Sheltering dripstones above the window developed into deeply carved label moulds. Tower-house windows were fitted with grilles of interthreaded iron bars.

Glass was the privilege of wealth in the middle ages. Ordinary folk closed their windows with screens of oiled parchment or wooden **shutters**, fitted to hinges or sliding in grooves on the inside face of the window frame. Glass became usual (at merchant level) during the sixteenth century — diamond-shaped grey-green panes, set in lead, fixed in frames, side-hung as opening casements or wired to a horizontal iron bar which crossed the mullions. Square-cut two-storeyed gabled bays broke the façade of lowland houses, glistering with green glass from sill to gable. Clear **crown glass**, glinting with arcing flaws and air bubbles, appeared during the seventeenth century. This affordable glass was fitted as rectangular panes

Casement window with label mould (above) and stone mullion, in Cotswold limestone, at Great Tew, Oxfordshire.

held by stout wooden glazing bars. Frames were fitted to slide horizontally (**Yorkshire sash**) or hinged to open as casements.

Tall rectangular window openings suited the higher ceilings of the seventeenth century, and **vertical sashes** (introduced about 1670) with multiple panes dominated the façades. By about 1740 the classic double-hung sash, shaped as a double square of twelve rectangular panes, dominated as the neo-classical orthodoxy. This formal style persisted until around 1840, glazing bars becoming ever more slender. Window spaces became a focus for decoration with rubbed-brick voussoirs and keystones above, panelled aprons below, raised

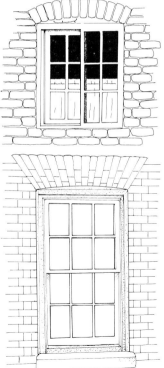

(Above left) Yorkshire (horizontally sliding) sash at Laxton, Nottinghamshire, about 1748.

(Left) Double-hung sash with twelve-pane glazing and rubbed-brick voussoir above; about 1850.

(Above) Corbridge, Northumberland. Datestones and other carved inscriptions offer valuable clues to the history of a house — its building, alteration and occupation. Here, a Latin motto — an improving commonplace ambiguously promising 'all good(s) to the good' — is dated 1707 (probably the year in which the house was built) and is accompanied by the initials of the first owner or occupier. The 1752 inscription is a marriage lintel or wedding window offering a further chapter in the history, comprising the initials of the husband and wife for whom this house was home. Research in marriage registers and title deeds is the essential follow-up to datestone clues. (Photograph: Cadbury Lamb.)

(Below left) Piended dormer window with householder's initials at Elgin, Moray, Grampian, about 1720.

(Below) Sash window with lying-pane glazing, a notable fashion around 1825-70, especially in Scotland: Elgin, about 1860.

margins, sills and soffits of contrasting stone. Alternative fashions flourished alongside the twelve-pane standard: the tripartite Venetian window, the round-headed Regency style, Gothick tracery. Bow windows protruded from polite façades after 1790 and the established order was turned on its side in the notable though short-lived lying-pane fashion (1825-70, chiefly in Scotland).

Sheet glass, available in large clear panes after 1840, lit interiors of every class. Glazing bars were cut away; twelve panes reduced to two. Bay windows (some with custom-made curved plate glass) became a standard feature of speculative suburbia (1860-1940). Arts and Crafts enthusiasts introduced stained glass into the home from about 1860 onwards: etched and coloured panes for the framing panels of Oxford glazing (1840-1910); richly allegorical leaded lights for a lobby or stair. Decor-

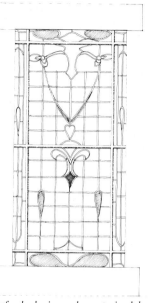

Oxford glazing: characterised by narrow framing panels, here with a display of stained glass in late Art Nouveau style at Elgin, Moray, Grampian, about 1902.

ative glass motifs enlightened all but the lowest social levels during the twentieth century, notably Art Nouveau (before 1914) and Art Déco (1920-50) for suburban fanlight or front door.

Water, gas and electricity

Water from pump, pond or well, maintained by parish, manor or borough, was supplemented from the 1830s by a supply from standpipes in the courts of the town. Running water was rarely piped beyond the kitchen before 1860. The bathtub before the fire was superseded from the 1880s by the separate bathroom with plumbed-in bath, lavatory (for hand washing), running hot and cold water and a selection of shower-bath options from the 1890s.

The **privy** over or near a cesspit (outdoor or indoor) and the sanitary earth closet (about 1860) were superseded by the flushing **water closet** connected to public sewer, cesspit or (1896) septic tank, and located in the smallest room — in the house or in the yard. The pan closet was flushed with water poured from a jug: the valve closet (in use 1770-1920) flushed automatically. The S-bend first appeared in the short hopper design, forerunner of the familiar one-piece earthenware washdown style (invented in the 1880s).

(Right) Thomas Lambert and Son's self-acting water closet, 1858, with seat removed to show the automatic flushing mechanism which was activated by the user's weight.

Gas was piped into urban homes for lighting from the 1840s. The gas cooker, copper and geyser appeared in the 1860s, gas fires around 1880.

The earliest public **electricity** supply lighted homes in Godalming, Surrey, in 1881. Electricity outshone oil and gas as well as supplying power to domestic appliances such as cooker (1894), heater (1897), refrigerator (1913) and washing machine (1914).

(Left) The typical dwelling of the modern movement reflected architectural theories of 'form determined by function' and 'the house as a machine for living in', realised in the starkly rectilinear 'moderne' façade, in smooth white render, and flat roofs. Large and metal-framed windows with horizontal glazing were often asymmetrically placed, even carried around an angle to break a vertical. The earliest British house in this 'international style' dates from the 1920s. This house on Sandbanks Road, Poole, is a fine exemplar, complete with (probably original) palm tree in the garden. (Photograph: John Barrett.)

7. Developing links

Medieval houses fitted neatly into plots planned, measured and pegged out by officials of the manor or the borough. In rural villages each house stood squarely on a broad tenement, perhaps fronting a communal green with its well or pond, maypole, cross, cucking stool, pound and stocks. In towns each burgess was allocated a burgage with a standard street frontage of some ten paces — broad enough for the merchant to build his house gable-end to the street. Access to the croft behind his house was by means of a pend (a covered passage) and a narrow alley (vennel, ginnel, wynd, twitten). As trade prospered the merchant added storerooms, workshops and journeymen's cottages which snaked down the reversed-S tail of the croft. The row was generally formed of structurally independent units abutting gable to gable. On the street façade too each property remained conspicuously aloof from its neighbour, if only by an inch or two, as burgesses jealously guarded against any blurring of boundary rights and avoided the legal and architectural complications of terraced living, party walls and unified façades.

New developments on virgin sites and ambitious schemes spreading across several burgages enabled imaginative builders from medieval times onwards to experiment with terraced housing, linking three or more dwellings within a unified scheme, with a (perhaps non-structural) party wall to divide house from house. Rows of almshouses, neat linked cottaging for the decent and deserving poor, pioneered the terrace fashion. Medieval streets also, occasionally, exhibit a coherent terraced front: eleven shops with solars erected for the merchants of Briggate, King's Lynn, Norfolk (1349); a neat range of wealden houses at Battle, East Sussex. From the seventeenth century onwards speculators developed greenfield sites with terraces of substantial houses. First-rate **terraces** were the basis of the rapid growth of suburban London: Bloomsbury Square (1660), St James's Square (1668), Golden Square (1670), Red Lion Square (1684), Soho Square (1681-90).

The grandeur of Georgian Bath and Edinburgh, of Regency Brighton and Victorian Glasgow was based upon the terrace — middle-class homes clustered together, the broad sweep of their combined façade aping the lordly colonnade of a magnate's palace, though even the most civilised front, such as Inigo Jones's Covent Garden piazza, might come, in time, to conceal a far from orderly interior of bagnios and brothels. The exclusivity of the square — and of its even more fashionable relatives, the crescent and circus (pioneered by John Wood at Bath in 1767-75) — was protected by gates and gate lodges. The houses gazed introspectively on to a

Bath, Avon. A first-rate terrace typical of the superior housing demanded by the upper classes from the eighteenth century onwards and built wherever wealth permitted, as for instance in Bath, Bloomsbury and Edinburgh. Often such houses were occupied during only the few weeks of each year when county families flocked to town for 'the season'. Principal reception rooms were usually located on the first floor, though decorative attention (window tracery, visual detail in stucco or stone, iron railings) was concentrated on the ground-floor façade. Sculleries, cellars, kitchens and servants' hall were relegated to basements. Servants slept in attics, their bedroom windows discreetly hidden by a balustrade or parapet. (Photograph: Cadbury Lamb.)

communal grassy space. In industrial settlements the terrace offered cost-effective housing and high-density land use in austere sweeps of stone barracking (such as the model settlement of New Lanark) and in rigid grids of streets spread across green fields in row upon row of identical back-to-backs, tunnel-backs and alley-backs, boxing in the working class under the shadow of the mill chimney, shipyard crane or pithead gear. Rural developers also seized upon the terrace style for estate villages. Landlords rebuilt in a style which advertised their own good taste, notably ranges of two-storeyed, four-roomed cottages for agricultural labourers dating from 1700 onwards.

Semi-detached cottages appeared in rural areas late in the seventeenth century. Polite architects developed the style for wealthy patrons with a taste for town planning. The village of Milton Abbas, Dorset, removed as an eyesore from the Earl of Dorchester's

North Street, Cromford, Derbyshire. This plain stone-built terrace was erected in 1777 for the workers of Sir Richard Arkwright, pioneer of the water-powered industrial cotton mill. The houses offered decent accommodation shaped to the needs of working men and their large families. The houses stand as austere memorials to the relationship between the patriarchal capitalist of the industrial revolution and his contented hands. Living accommodation was confined to the ground and first floors. On the second floor an attic room ran the length of the terrace and here, lighted by long low windows, craftsmen worked, manufacturing stockings from cotton spun by machines in the mill. (Photograph: David Iredale.)

(Above left) Second-rate terraced house: pattern-book design by M. A. Nicholson, 1836, of a classic town house for a wealthy upper middle-class family.

(Above right) Fourth-rate terraced house: pattern-book design by M. A. Nicholson, 1836, of a typical town house for the family of a prospering city clerk.

park, was rebuilt about 1771-90 as forty semi-detached cottages, 'pert white thatched boxes', spaced along a sinuous tree-lined street laid out by 'Capability' Brown. The semi arrived in town with the suburban boom of the early nineteenth century, notably with the Eyre Estate, St John's Wood, London.

For convenience, and as a boast of wealth, house and farm buildings might be linked in a continuous range: in-line, L-shape, open-square, double-square. This association is the badge of the independent farmer, working an anciently enclosed fieldscape in the south-west or a parliamentary enclosure in the midlands and north. The style and accommodation of the domestic unit supplies the researcher's chief clues as to date. In-line **house and byre** 'longhouses' were erected in Devon until around 1700, men and beasts sharing a common crosspassage entrance. In Cumbria house

Semi-detached houses at Ampthill, Bedfordshire, 1815: close studding with brick nogging; the original doorways were in the gable ends; the right-hand house of the pair has been improved with a front door.

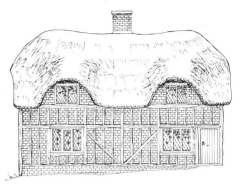

and byre 'statesmen's houses' became widespread during the late seventeenth century. Yorkshire house and barn/byre **laithe houses** (from the mid seventeenth century onwards, but generally from the late eighteenth century) presented a David and Goliath aspect, the house dwarfed by the barn/byre (laithe). House, barn and byre possessed separate entrances, the laithe door constructed as a lofty arch, high enough to admit a loaded hay sled. Laithe houses were built into the nineteenth century, later examples occupied by small-holders working recent enclosures on marginal land.

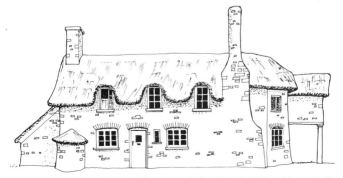

Vernacular house at Allerford, Somerset, built of local rubble with externally projecting bread oven, with round front chimney stack typical of south-west England; improved with lean-to (penthouse) extension, porch and additional square chimney.

8. Aspect

A house wears its identity in its face: literally in a datestone or marriage lintel; more subtly in the general aspect of the structure. Vernacular houses grow naturally from the landscape: mellow brick the colour of new-ploughed soil; ragged rubble outcropping from bouldery pasture. The medieval and vernacular house presents an irregular aspect, its doors and windows located with regard to internal convenience rather than external coherence. Ovens bulge asymmetrically from kitchen walls; porches, ends and outshuts enliven the plan; chimneys rise in top-heavy discord above steeply pitched, broadly sweeping rooflines with unconcerted dormers and gables.

Renaissance architects imposed classical concepts of symmetry and concord. Neo-classical taste required the harmonious balance of elements: a focal front door flanked by ranks of regular repetitious windows; a strict geometry of cubes and rectangles defined by frieze, entablature, pilaster, coping, cornice and balustrade. The seats of the gentry assumed the neo-classical manners of Palladio and parodied the pedimented temples of Greece and Rome, while the lodge at the park gate, the keeper's house and even the stables sported correct twelve-pane sashes and a pedimented portico. The classic red-brick house with white stone dressings crowned by slated roof developed from the seventeenth century onwards as a style for manor house and urbane terrace, for modest farmhouse and workman's cottage.

Eighteenth-century romantics revived and reinvented Gothic style — borrowing features from medieval church and castle and enriching their houses with ivy-clad towers, lancets, merlons, crockets and crenellations, while the *cottage orné* nestled among the shrubberies — snug home for dowager or tenant. Restrained Gothic spread its influence down the social scale: fussy tracery in a window sash, picturesque bargeboards, moulded mullions, an iron-studded door.

A rash of new styles entered the architectural vocabulary, such as the Italianate style — low-pitched roofs, campanile towers, stucco cornices and scrolled brackets. Villa and terrace affected aspects of Ruritanian castle, Moghul pavilion, Gallic *château* and Alpine chalet. The first **bungalows** appeared (at Westgate, Kent, in 1869) as holiday homes. Prefabricated versions were marketed from the 1880s as desirable weekend cottages. Middle-class bungalows — comfortable, single-storeyed, covered by a pagoda-profile roof, fronted by a veranda — punctuated the villa developments on the edges of towns from the 1890s. After 1918 brick bungalow dream homes sprawled across suburbia.

Native traditional styles were revived from the 1860s. Red brick and rubble were revered as a virtuous vernacular, no longer to be concealed by stucco and plaster. Tudor-style chimney stacks, crow-steps, dormers and projecting gables disrupted the roofline. A rambling plan was complemented by irregular fenestration, Jacobethan bays and rustic porches. The ideals of Arts and Crafts architects were, however, a costly luxury, and clients compromised, accepting mass-produced iron guttering, stock brick, terracotta

Tollhouse built at Sutterton, Lincolnshire, as a cottage orné — a style particularly in vogue 1790-1820.

chimney pots and ridge tiles. Moreover, building regulations governing lighting, ventilation, ceiling height, sanitation, structure and accommodation further restricted vernacular usage — of materials (cob, thatch, timber) and traditional plans. R. Norman Shaw (1831-1912) realised a Queen Anne style (hipped roofs, tile hanging, dormers, Dutch gables, pargeting and red brick) for middle-class homes on the Bedford Park estate, a countrified Kentish ambience translated to Chiswick in west London. Vernacular revival architects designed the sylvan sprawl of speculative and semi-detached suburbia, 1880-1939; model villages such as Port Sunlight in the Wirral (begun in 1890 for Lever's soap workers) and Bournville in Birmingham (1898, for Cadbury employees); garden cities (Letchworth, Hertfordshire, 1903, designed by Raymond Unwin and Barry Parker); garden suburbs (Hampstead, London, 1908, by Edwin Lutyens); and estates of council housing following the act of 1919.

Double-pile prefabricated bungalow, about 1928, sold by David Ross and Sons, Forres, Moray, Grampian, price £175 carriage paid.

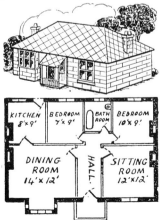

59

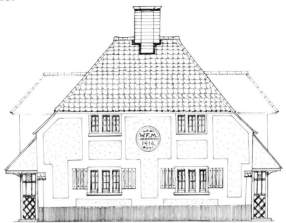

Rural semi-detached houses in vernacular revival style, Essex type, designed by Holland W. Hobbiss (an architect's pseudonym adopted for a competition entry); plans published by the Board of Agriculture and Fisheries, 1914.

Houses of the modern movement from the first decades of the twentieth century exhibit stark rectilinear forms — cool white cement, flat roofs and metal-framed windows. Modernist style influenced suburban and ribbon developments, particularly in southern England, in the period 1925-39, and infected public housing after 1945 as planners, architects and governments conspired in a brave new world of new towns and tower blocks.

The startling geometry of the modern movement: bungalow designed by J. and W. Wittet, Elgin, 1947.

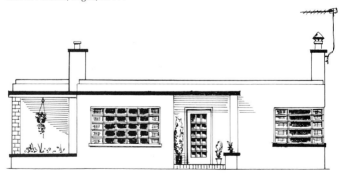

9. Libraries

Research now moves indoors, into the public library and local studies centre, before expanding outwards through the inter-library loans network and into the university libraries and national institutions (British Library, *et cetera*). In addition to the books displayed on library shelves there are supporting collections in reserve stock and closed access stacks, as well as accumulations of newspapers, microfilms, special collections, maps, plans, theses, pamphlets, handbills and manuscripts.

Basic **textbooks** offer a primary education in architecture (vernacular and polite) — an understanding of form and function, building technique, style, terms, detail and historical development. General theses contain references to specific buildings — perhaps to the researcher's own house — or to influential strains of design from which thousands of houses are descended. A seminal *Essay on British Cottage Architecture* by James Malton, 1798, defined vernacular architecture ('the peculiar mode of building which was originally the effect of chance').

Architectural **pattern books**, published from the eighteenth century onwards, enshrined current concepts of taste in exemplary building plans, elevations and details. Pattern books offer clues to the date of actual buildings, especially where designs were directly plagiarised, particularly those of William Halfpenny, John Wood the younger, John Soane, Richard Elsam and J. C. Loudon. More usually, though, pattern-book concepts were filtered through the practical mason's realisation (or misunderstanding) of the principles demonstrated, and his client's whim. Handbooks for the guidance of craftsmen supply the present-day researcher with a valuable basis for dating a house from the style of details — door, architrave, wainscot, baluster, voussoir, moulding, *et cetera*.

Guides to the housing and architecture of the locality might begin with a sixteenth-century perambulation:

> part of Thames street ... called Galley row, but more commonly Petty Wales ... these buildings ... hath fallen to ruin, and been let out for stabling of horses, to tipplers of beer, and such like; amongst others, one Mother Mampudding (as they termed her) for many years kept this house, or a great part thereof, for victualling; and it seemeth that the builders of the hall of this house were shipwrights, and not house carpenters; for the frame thereof (being but low) is raised of certain principal posts of main timber, fixed deep in the ground, without any groundsell, boarded close round about on the inside, having none other wall from the ground to the roof, those boards not exceeding the length of a clap board, about an inch thick, every board ledging over

other as in a ship or galley, nailed with ship nails called rough and clench.
(J. Stow. *A Survay of London ... Written in the Yeare 1598.* Dent, 1912, pages 123-4.)

Tourist guides and **gazetteers** offer revealing vignettes based upon observation and local tradition:

Old Mason Lodge ... on the north side of High Street, is a two-storey thatched house, with crow-stepped gable to the street ... was at one time devoted to the meetings of the mystic brethren, and now belongs to a family of the name of Fridge. A pedimented panel in the south gable bears the initials 'A.F.', 'M.R.', with a rose in the centre and date 1660.
(J. and W. Watson. *Morayshire Described Being a Guide to Visitors.* Elgin, 1868, pages 264-5.)

Local histories notice houses:

Little Mitton ... The basement story is of stone, and part of the upper ditto of wood; the pasterns, however, descending perpendicularly to the ground, and resting on pedestals of stone. The hall, with its embayed window, screen and gallery over ... the roof is ceiled with oak in wrought compartments; the principals turned in the form of obtuse Gothic arches ... the walls covered with wainscot, and the bay window adorned with armorial bearings in painted glass
(T. Whitaker. *An History of the Original Parish of Whalley.* Blackburn, 1801, page 237.)

The print accompanying this description differs significantly from a view later drawn by Nathaniel Philips in 1824. George Shaw, the antiquarian, recorded impressions of Mitton on 8th March 1833. Much of what he described (such as the stained glass) was later torn out, though the removal of wall plastering later revealed early sixteenth-century window openings.

a fine old building, but gradually sinking into a state of decay. — The hall ... is immense, and open to the roof which rests on splendidly carved beams and spandrels. The walls are wainscotted to the roof, and the skreen is gorgeous. This magnificent room is lighted by an oriel which contains some armorial bearings in stained glass ... In the yard is a stone coffin used as a pig trough
(Manchester Local History Library, MS.927.2 S15.)

The Victoria History of the Counties of England (VCH) contains chapters on the architecture and housing of each parish with notice of specific developments:

The house at Edgwarebury is mentioned in 1548, and a house and farm buildings are shown on the map of 1597, north and east of the pond. The existing house on the site, known as Bury Farm, has an older portion which probably dates from the early 17th century; this is partly timber-framed with external weather-boarding and a jettied upper story ... Dick Turpin is said to have stolen the silver, raped the daughter of the householder, and poured boiling water over her father.
(VCH. *A History of the County of Middlesex* volume IV, 1971, page 157.)

Vernaculár architecture as an academic pursuit came of age with the Royal Commission on Historical Monuments volume *Dorset I* (researched 1930s, published 1952) and the seminal *Monmouthshire Houses* by C. Fox and Lord Raglan (Welsh Folk Museum, Cardiff, 1951-4).

The popular *The Buildings of England* and *Buildings of Scotland* series (edited and founded by N. Pevsner) notice churches, public buildings, mansions and humbler houses which took the writer's eye. The *Architectural Guides to Scotland* series (Royal Incorporation of Architects in Scotland) describes domestic buildings at all social levels in such architectural regions as *Clackmannan* and *Stirling and the Trossachs*.

Printed **directories** from the seventeenth century (London) and the eighteenth century (provincial towns) are guides to local people, places and institutions, which may permit the history of a house to be traced through a succession of occupants and owners. Among the most comprehensive and accurate of nineteenth-century directories are those of Kelly (the Post Office London directory), Baines, White, Pigot, Slater and Bagshaw. Professional directories may reveal the callings practised in the researcher's home, incidentally tracing the ebb and flow of a neighbourhood's prosperity.

Miss MOFFAT, *alias* BEESTON, *Fountain-closs*.
THIS Lady is tall, black complexion, and about 30 years of age. She is very artful in her amours, and is almost worn out in the service. However, it is said, she does her business extremely well, as she still likes to mumble a piece of grisle.
(*Ranger's Impartial List of the Ladies of Pleasure in Edinburgh.* Edinburgh, 1775, page 28.)

Newspapers in recognisable modern form appeared in London during the seventeenth century, spawning a swelling number of provincial imitators, including the *Worcester Post-man* (1690) and the *Belfast News-letter* (1737, the earliest Irish title). Particularly useful to the historian of houses are advertisements by developers for tenders — for work by carpenters, masons, plumbers, thatchers, *et cetera* — while notices of sale reveal forgotten place-names, long-lost occupiers' names, significant former uses of sites and houses, and conditions of tenure:

> TO BE SOLD ... at the SPREADEAGLES IN WREXHAM ... A Dwelling-house in Abbot-street, late in the holding of John Jones; containing a large dining-room, two parlours, a kitchen, scullery, pantry, larder, and brew-house, six good lodging-rooms, a vault 34 feet long by 16 wide; very convenient for carrying on the wine business
> (*Chester Chronicle*, 5th December 1777.)

Periodical publications, from the eighteenth century onwards, were tailored to specific markets; for instance, professional journals such as *The Builder* (1842) discussed latest developments of interest to the trade.

Literary works inevitably describe houses and their occupants. The novelist roots fiction in identifiable neighbourhoods. The poet portrays the built environment, albeit coloured by his own perception. The diarist idealises his tranquil home and the traveller depicts the places she visits:

> Adison Bank, the houses lookes just like the booths at a fair ... they have no chimneys their smoke comes out all over the house ... there is no roome in their houses but is up to the thatch and in which are 2 or 3 beds even to their parlours and buttery; and notwithstanding the cleaning of their parlour for me I was not able to bear the roome.
> (*The Illustrated Journeys of Celia Fiennes 1685-c.1712*, edited by C. Morris, London and Exeter, 1982, page 173.)

The extensive archival resources of libraries and record offices (national and local) may be exploited in the comfort of the researcher's local public library in print, typescript and microfilm. The published guides to county, borough and public record offices whet the appetite with a taste of documentary feasts for the future. An hors-d'oeuvre to the archives includes offprints of minutes and reports of conservation societies on individual houses; microfilmed census returns from 1841 onwards; parish registers recording inhabitants and their dwellings; published calendars and copies of administrative records of the national government such as inquisitions *post mortem*; and surveys of monastic property confiscated, 1536-9, and of royalist dwellings sequestrated or compounded for, 1644-57. Of the Parliamentary Civil Survey (1654-6) of Ireland only parts of Leinster, Munster and Ulster survive:

City of Limerick, parish of St Nicholas
Nicholas ffanyng of Lymericke Alderman Irish Papist ... A tworth
stone house next on the north to the former House of Andrew
Creaghs and the high Street on the west ... Two Cadgworke Houses
thereunto adioyning on the east with a passadge betwixt them, wh a
Backside ... Another House of stone & Clay ... owing for langable
Rent to the Corporation 9*d* yearely
(*The Civil Survey*, edited by R. C. Simington, Dublin, Stationery
Office, 1931-61, volume IV, page 440.)

Historical and antiquarian societies sponsor **editions** of local and
national records:

10.1528 May 18. Sasine on precept of chancery, in favour of Patrick
Creichtoun, as son and heir of the late Patrick Creichtoun of
Cranstoun Riddaill, of a back-land, under and above, with halls,
chambers, cellars and houses thereof, in which James McCalzeane
now dwells; together with the kitchen above the close and pend, with
all their pertinents, lying on the north side of the High Street, within
a tenement of the late William Cranston of Rathobyres, between the
foreland of the said late William on the south, and a land of the late
William Adamson on the north.
(*Protocol Book of John Foular 1528-1534*, edited by J. Durham,
Scottish Record Society, new series 10 [1985], page 4.)

Select **records of Parliament** (original archives at the House of
Lords Record Office), prime sources for the study of housing, may
be available in print (as published blue books), photographic re-
prints or microform at larger reference libraries. Sessional papers
(returns to committees of the Lords or Commons, annual or occa-
sional reports of government departments, reports of royal commissions of inquiry, private or public bill papers, *et cetera*) refer to
housing in general and to properties in particular, for example the
royal commissions on the housing of the working classes, 1884-5,
and on land in Wales, 1894-6. Acts of the parliaments of England,
Ireland and Scotland (public and private) refer to houses, notably
in general guidelines for builders for fire or sanitary purposes.
London building acts from 1666 onwards specified permitted
materials (brick, stone, stucco, lead, iron) and set structural standards for each of seven rates of house. In 1707 regulations declared
'no Mundillion or Cornish of Timber ... be made' and that brick
parapets 'be carried two foot and an half high above the Garret
Floor' — a fire precaution measure which influenced urban architecture throughout Britain for a century or more.
The **Royal Commissions on Historical Monuments** (founded
1908 for Scotland, Wales and England) record, analyse and assess

ancient and historical monuments and buildings, and compile, curate and make available promiscuous accumulations of photographs, plans, reports and inventories, including items not accessible through the public library service. Architectural records include notebooks and reports of peripatetic commission surveyors, original architectural accounts and plans from the eighteenth century onwards, surveys of threatened buildings (from 1968), and the register of historic buildings under the Survey of London (founded 1894). Commission publications include summary reports on buildings; scholarly county tomes inventorying buildings most worthy of preservation; studies of a particular limited area or type of structure; national textbooks such as *Houses of the Welsh Countryside* and *English Vernacular Houses.*

Falkland, Fife, a royal burgh by virtue of its proximity to a royal palace (1501 onwards), is now dominated by a linoleum factory (1931). The pantile roofs of these eighteenth-century harled stone houses are typical of eastern counties and a notable vernacular in Fife. The forestairs of these dwellings exemplify several themes in Scottish domestic architecture. The first-floor hall house had its living rooms (entered by a separate outside stair) above a store or shop. Conversely a ground-floor dwelling might have a separate store, workroom or net-drying loft above (reached by a separate outside stair). Forestairs and stair turrets, added to the façades of properties, narrowed burgh high streets as inhabitants went in for two-storey living from the sixteenth century onwards. Outside stairs (forestairs and turrets) were an essential feature of tenements. (Photograph: David Iredale.)

10. Pictures and prints, plats and plans

Pictures bring the past to life, depicting a house in the liveries and conditions of several generations, portraying the occupants who made the house a home. But pictures seldom tell the whole truth. The artist, to please a patron or to satisfy a convention, drew in architecture of tasteful elegance or charming rusticity but painted out the unaesthetic pigsties and hovels which cluttered the prospect. Alternatively, pictorial propagandists (such as Hogarth and Doré) might prefer to emphasise the dilapidation and squalor of the scene. Even the camera could lie: the long exposures of early photography, the harsh glare of magnesium flare and electronic flash, rendered interiors (specially tidied for the occasion) brighter and cheerier than dense net curtains, gas light, smoking grates and dirty windows ever allowed.

From the twelfth century the **bird's-flight view** (map view, plan view) surveyed landscape in plan but pictured buildings in elevation (though not to scale). The prospect of a town, village or mansion took its view from ground level. The **bird's-eye view** depicted landscapes in perspective from a high oblique angle. The majority of views remained in manuscript, particularly those produced for a specific purpose or patron. Views commissioned for military purposes, such as those along the south coast of England or records of sieges in the plantation of Ireland, might be retained by government officials (frequently among their own family muniments), whence they were eventually transmitted to national collections and local record offices.

Printed views (woodcuts, etchings, lithographs and engravings) were issued as broadsheets, book illustrations or details for topographical maps, exploiting a growing market from the late fifteenth century onwards. Among the earliest published representations of British towns are views and picture-maps of sieges, fortifications and naval actions, printed and sold to satisfy public curiosity. Between 1572 and 1618 was published G. Braun (editor) and F. Hogenberg (engraver), *Civitates Orbis Terrarum*, an atlas of 546 town views and prospects, based upon surveys conducted 1560-1611. London was mapped in the *Civitates* style by Norden (1600), Hondius (about 1611), Visscher (1616) and Merian (1638). John Speed, *The Theatre of the Empire of Great Britaine*, 1611-12, depicted over seventy towns in bird's-flight view. The swansong of the aerial townscape was John Cossins's (1725) bird's-flight over Leeds.

While the pictorial map withered during the seventeenth century, pictorial prints flourished, for instance the *Theatrum Scotiae* of

John Slezer (1693), *Britannia Illustrata* of Johannes Kip (1708) and the collected *Antiquities and Venerable Remains* of S. and N. Buck (1774). Underpinning the work of these national figures was a busy host of nameless or obscure artists and engravers whose pictures are preserved in library, archive, art gallery and museum, in published histories, guides and gazetteers, and on drawing-room walls throughout the locality. And lithographs and engravings of premises graced hotel menus; representations of factories, shops, streetscapes and model estates boasted of capitalist enterprise on company stationery, while friezes of notable architecture graced the borders of published plans.

From the 1840s onwards amateur and professional **photographers** froze the static landscapes of town and country on to daguerreotype, calotype, collodion and glass plate. Fast-exposure cameras and film negative introduced candid shots of the family at home, supplementing stiff portraits posed before a painted studio backdrop. From the 1890s a photographer was present at most public occasions — photographing commemorative tree-plantings and proclamations of kings — incidentally capturing backgrounds of thatched roofs and smoking chimneys, of children and parlour maids enjoying a grandstand view from the nursery window. **Moving pictures** from 1893 onwards (in colour from 1906) and video (from the 1970s) offered further opportunities for capturing lively images of house and home. From about 1900 effective photographic half-tone illustrations appeared in newspapers and magazines. The **picture postcard** industry flourished from the 1860s under the leadership of entrepreneurs such as James Valentine of Dundee and Francis Frith of Reigate: the Frith company archive (300,000 photographs in 1970) was published as 67 microfiche volumes in 1988.

Air photographs offer dramatic images of a house in context — in relation to both the landscape of the present and the relics of the past (the cropmarks and soilmarks of prehistoric barrow, henge, pit and dyke; the humps, holloways and house platforms of deserted settlement on the site). The significant collections held by the Cambridge University Committee for Aerial Photography are supplemented by private archives (such as that of Hunting Aerofilms of Borehamwood, Hertfordshire) and local and national government records. Luftwaffe photographs (1939-40, now in United States National Archives, Washington) present images of southeast England before the post-war redevelopment. Ordnance Survey and Royal Air Force aerial photographs are available for research in the relevant National Monuments Record.

A **plan** represents the landscape schematically and symbolically, as if viewed from directly above, and at uniform scale. Correct spatial relationships are observed and the dimensions of a house may thus be ascertained by admeasurement and calculation using the scale. Printed plans at useful scale, in the accepted modern style, were issued for towns from the eighteenth century onwards, exemplified in Rocque's Bristol (1742), Scalé's Waterford (1764), Green's Manchester and Salford (1787-94), Hochstetter's Norwich (1789) and Horwood's London (1799). A comprehensive collection of settlement plans was published (and to a large extent surveyed) by John Wood in his atlas (1828) of 48 Scottish towns. A profitable market for printed county maps spurred surveyors to develop cartographic techniques and to work at scales of 1 or 2 inches to the mile, large enough to indicate individual houses in rural districts. Joel Gascoyne's Cornwall (fourteen sheets, about 1700) was the first, emulated by William Williams's Denbigh and Flint (about 1720), J. Noble and J. Keenan's County Kildare (1752), G. Yates's Glamorgan (1799) and C. and J. Greenwood's county maps (1817-34).

The **Ordnance Survey** originated in military mapping of the troublesome Celtic fringes of the kingdom. From 1747 to 1755 William Roy prepared a 1:36,000 'Great Map' of Scotland, depicting a landscape of cottages, clachans and common fields on the eve of clearance. In 1784 Roy moved south to fix a base line at Hounslow for the first 1 inch (1:63,360) Ordnance Survey of England and Wales. The published maps were reduced from 6 inch or 25 inch manuscript surveys (now preserved in the British Library). Scottish and Irish 1 inch maps (derived from larger-scale surveys) appeared from 1843 and 1855 respectively. Ordnance Survey 6 inch (1:10,560) mapping commenced in Ireland with County Londonderry (published 1833), finishing with Kerry in 1846. 6 inch mapping was introduced in mainland Britain from the 1840s. 25 inch Ordnance Survey plans (1:2500, 25.344 inches to 1 mile) commenced in Durham in 1853, eventually covering all except marginal or uncultivated land. This large scale permitted the inclusion of fine detail such as the bay windows of a house and the privy in the garden. A book of reference accompanied the first edition 25 inch plan indicating land use, field names and acreages. A general revision of the 6 and 25 inch maps was completed between 1891 and 1913; a partial third edition was abandoned in 1922. Ordnance Survey town plans began with a manuscript plan at 1:2640 of Derry (1827). Published plans at larger scales — variously 1:500 (10.56 feet to 1 mile) and 1:1056 (5 feet to 1 mile) — commenced with Dublin (1840-8). The survey in England commenced with St Helens (1843-4), subsequently mapping towns in Britain with populations exceeding 4000 between 1855 and 1894. These richly detailed plans show exact ground plans of houses with their bays, bows, porches and conservatories — and even the layout of statuary, shrubberies and individual trees in the garden. Unpublished Ordnance Survey archives for England, Wales and Scotland were lost in the bombing of Southampton in 1940. However, Irish records survive in Dublin as a feast of supplementary information: manuscript plans 1825-42; memoranda; antiquity plans; field and town name-books (place-names); and O'Donovan's maps of County Antrim, superimposing the seventeenth-century 'down' survey on the current 6 inch map.

In England and Wales an act of 1836 permitted the commutation of church tithes paid in kind into money payments in parishes where this process was not already accomplished. (Midland counties had generally commuted tithes on enclosure.) A surveyor drew a plan at large scale, individually numbering each parcel of land, house and outbuilding in the parish. An apportionment recorded the names of owners and occupiers as well as description, acreage and state of cultivation. Three copies of the **tithe plan** were prepared, now to be sought in parish chest and county, diocesan or public record office. Irish tithe applotment books at the Public Record Office of Ireland are comprehensive parish word-surveys for the period 1825-37, identifying the plots of land on which tithes were paid.

Baile, Loch Watersee, Isle of Berneray. The blackhouse was constructed throughout the Hebrides from the 1780s. The drystone walls were of double thickness with a peat core. The straw or heather thatch was secured by weighted ropes. Originally an open fire provided heating but chimneys were later added and interiors were divided to create a two-and-a-half room or a two-and-a-half-plus-one room layout. (Photograph: David Iredale.)

11. Doing the deeds

Title deeds to a house typically comprise a fat bundle of legal documents properly tied with red tape — a promiscuous collection of conveyances, leases, bonds, mortgages, marriage contracts, actions for eviction, wills, maps, plans, building warrants and certificates of completion. The deed bundle may be held by the householder or his solicitor. Deeds to a rented house are held by the landlord or his agent. If the house is subject to a mortgage, deeds must be sought with the relevant bank or building society, from whom photocopies are obtainable. Older deeds to a property carved out of a larger land unit may remain in the possession of the original owner (a landed estate, property developer, urban landlord, local authority, nationalised industry, *et cetera*). The new deed created when a fragment of an estate was thus sold may quote the evidence of relevant predecessor deeds in an abstract of title or a 'whereas' clause. On 8th May 1820 John Sevier of Lymington, mariner, sold a 'parcel of garden ground Messuage or Tenement' to Edward May of Lymington, builder. A whereas clause narrated the history of the land: before 1796 the garden 'had then sometime since been inclosed ... out of the waste of [Old Lymington] Manor at King's Saltern green'; on 23rd September 1796 'All that new erected Messuage Tenement or Dwellinghouse and Outhouses erected and built by the said John Sevier' was formally leased to him by the lady of the manor; around 1818 Sevier had 'lately erected and built another Messuage or Tenement and Kitchen and Room over the same' (Cheshire Record Office, Birch Cullimore papers).

A medieval messuage (house and land associated) held in **fee simple** was enjoyed on condition of performing services to the superior lord(s). These services and profitable incidents of tenure attached to the feu (property), rather than the person. The lord was therefore interested in every feudal transfer, preferably by **public livery of seisin** (handing over of possession). On completion of their financial transaction, buyer (feoffee) and seller visited the site in company of witnesses (including perhaps a representative of the feudal superior), whereupon a symbolic stick, stone or turf was handed over to signify enfeoffment and the feoffee actually entered into any buildings. No written deed was required in England until 1677, and a freehold could not legally be transferred by deed without livery of seisin until reforms of 1833-45.

Written evidence was obviously useful, and from the twelfth century took the form of **charters of feoffment** (formal transfers of possession) or deeds of gift. Following the example of royal writs, the charter was a missive in Latin issued by a grantor and addressed openly 'to all men both present and to come' (*sciant presentes et futuri*). The medieval feoffment recorded a complete transaction and thus incorporated the operative words 'have given, granted and confirmed' (*dedi concessi et hac presenti carta mea confirmavi*). The charter, a deed poll (executed in person and cut square at the head), alluded to monetary or other considerations: *pro viginti et quatuor solidis sterlingorum* ('for £24 sterling'). The ensuing 'habendum' clause specified the nature and extent of the feoffee's interest:

> *Habendum et tenendum totum predictum tenementum cum omnibus pertinenciis suis prefato X et heredibus suis uel suis assignatis de capitalibus dominis feodi in perpetuum.* ('To have and to hold all the said tenement with all its appurtenancies to the said X [grantee] and his heirs or his assigns of the chief lords of the fee in perpetuity'.)

The words of limitation 'his heirs' denoted a conveyance in fee simple, the most complete interest enjoyed in common law. The following 'reddendum' clause concerned annual services customarily due, which, to prevent the financial losses of subinfeudation, were reserved, after 1290, to the superior (chief lord) rather than to the grantor. The warranty protected the purchaser, whose rights might be subsequently attacked. The charter was sealed by the warrantor (seller), witnessed and dated. A memorandum of livery of seisin might be endorsed.

In Scotland a notary public's written instrument of **sasine** commenced with the words: 'In the Name of God Amen be it evidentlie knowen to all men':

> instrument of sasine in favour of John Lesslie air in speciall ... to ... Mr John Lesslie of Midletown his father ... all and Haill ... part ... of the deceast John Kay Burges of Elgin his for house or forland ... sometyme possest be the deceast Robert Shipheird merchant there Comprehending therin the Hall within the Turn pick door chamber within the same above ... John Kay his gate wherby they enter to his roods ... with the loft above the said hall and forshop under the Samen adjacent to the eastmost cheek of the said gate ... 3 June 1698 (J. R. Barrett, Elgin, 23/2.)

An assurance of title in the absence of registration of deeds or following loss of a charter bundle might be sought through court action. From the twelfth century to 1833 the final concord (**fine**) was a conveyance based upon a feigned action at law wherein an agreement under court auspices was colluded on ownership: *haec est finalis concordia* ('this is the final agreement'). The fine recited the whole property (messuages, cottages, orchards, *et cetera*) of the plaintiff (perhaps an intending purchaser) and conceded his title against the deforceant (grantor). The fine, assuming any form the parties and court chose, was employed for various purposes: to bar all claims to the property after five years (even if the title deeds were otherwise defective), as a married woman's conveyance or to facilitate family settlements and mortgages, as a preliminary to levying a recovery, and as a standard security measure in favour of a purchaser. The court record was written out three times on a single parchment, the texts separated by the word *chirographum*, 'handwriting'. The texts were separated by zigzag cuts through the authenticating word, for the archives of the court, conusee (plaintiff) and deforceant (conusor). The conusee's copy should be retained in the deed bundle to a property, the court copy (the *pes* or foot) at the Public Record Office.

A stronger assurance of title until 1833, because it was based on a judgement of court (rather than collusive agreement), was the **common recovery**. The plaintiff won his property from the respondent, whose vouchee(s) to warranty deserted him (and the court) and was adjudged in contempt. The plaintiff recovered his property from the wrongful possessor; the respondent sought compensation (in vain) from the vouchee, a man of no means (perhaps court crier). The recovery might bar a wife's dower, convey land free from a leasehold term, defeat restrictions upon mortmain (concerning ecclesiastical property) and (particularly from 1471) bar an entail (free land from strict descent to heirs). An exemplification of recovery commenced with the names of the king and his justices, the date of the law term, and the county. Richard Rowe, Hugh Hunt, Edward House, *et cetera*, were conventional names assumed for vouchees and common disseisors (dispossessors).

In certain towns, as security against fire, flood or fraud — and especially where local customary right allowed bequeathing of land by will — a burgess might ask the town clerk to copy his title deeds, leases, testaments and contracts into the borough court book; or he lodged the original deed itself for safe keeping in the town clerk's files. Borough authorities also established formal **registries** as a service to the lieges, for instance at Winchester in 1303. Notaries public in Scotland maintained protocol books for the enrolment of deeds. Landowners (particularly the nobility, church and crown) registered legal documents — charters, grants, leases, excambions (exchanges), *et cetera* — in their own chartularies (collections of charters).

illud mesuagiu[m] quod vocat[ur] mulleberyhall in Stayngat in Ciuitat[e] Ebor[aci] cu[m] om[n]ib[us] domib[us] sup[er]edificatis

... iacet in longitudi[n]e a Regia strata de Stayngat ante vsq[ue] ad venella[m] que vocat[ur] Grapecuntlane ret[r]o. [et] in latitudine int[er] ten[ementum] Prior[is] s[an]c[t]i Oswaldi ex p[ar]te occident[ali] [et] ten[ementum] Ric[ard]i de Seleby ex p[ar]te orientali
(York Minster Library, M2/4g f26v, capitular register, 4 February 1342/1343)

The corporation administering the reclaimed fenland of the Bedford Level required registration of deeds concerning property transactions within the level, from 1663 until abolition in 1920. Sasines (Scottish for seisin) registers were opened for Scottish shires from 1617 (1681 for burghs) — now deposited in local record offices and the Scottish Record Office. An Irish act of 1707 established a national registry accepting leases, mortgages, conveyances and settlements — though not leases for under 21 years, the tenure permitted to papists. County registries were established in Middlesex and the three ridings of Yorkshire under acts of Parliament of 1704, 1707, 1708 and 1735. In 1862 Parliament established a voluntary national land registry, though this proved ineffective except in London, where registration became compulsory: enquiries can be made to district land registries or to the central office, Lincoln's Inn Fields, London WC2A 3PH.

Lawyers attempted to remedy obstructions to property transfer through uses, regarding the beneficial estate (use) as personal property grantable by deed and separate from the legal estate (tenure). The resultant **feoffment to uses** whereby A conveyed a property to XYZ to hold to the use of A or a third party B, enabled A (the *cestui que use*) to evade feudal incidents, knight service, vows of poverty and prohibitions against devising property by will, on the grounds that XYZ (the feoffees to uses) were the legal tenants in fee simple, liable for services — though not in possession of the estate. Under chancery protection the *cestui que use* (beneficiary) could sell off portions of the property through feoffees, create family settlements, subject tenements to the use declared by will, and dispose of the use to others by deed of grant. The act concerning uses and wills (27 Henry VIII chapter X, 1535) executed the use into a legal estate in possession, bypassing the feoffees to uses, and giving the *cestui que use* the fee simple. The use no longer served its original purposes. The statute, in recognising the use in common law, opened the way to the creation of various future estates through grants to uses. From the seventeenth century to 1926 grants in the form of a use upon a use (unto and to the use of XYZ to the use of — upon trust for — A) created a legal estate for XYZ (trustees) and equitable interests for A. This was a basis of modern equitable ownership and the relationship of trustee and beneficiary. To avoid abuse, the act of inrollment of bargains and sales (27 Henry VIII chapter XVI, 1535) required deposit of deeds with the clerk of the peace or a court of law at Westminster from 1st July 1536 (enrolled copies substitute for deeds lost from the houseowner's bundle). The bargain and sale, an indenture (deed and counterpart engrossed on one parchment, and then divided by an indented cut) was an agreement between two parties. The deed included recitals ('whereas' clause), 'habendum', 'reddendum', and covenant to exhibit earlier deeds retained by the vendor. The operative words were 'hath granted bargained and sold'. The bargain and sale, though disadvantageous in, for example, not barring contingent remainders and not creating settlements or trusts, was the usual conveyance in the sixteenth and seventeenth centuries:

> bargain and sale: Robert Wyncott of Whicheforde, Warwickshire, gentleman, to Thomas Huyck of Arches howse and sometyme called Mountioye place in the p[ar]ishe of St Bennett next Powles wharf, London, doctor at law ... for £40 ... All that messuage or tenemente ... called the whyte lyon scituate and beinge in the strete called St Johns strete withoute the barres of west Smythfelde in the suburbes of London and in the p[ar]ishe of St Sepulchre withowte newgate of London nowe or late in the tenure or occupac[i]on of Margarett Hollingeshedd widowe ... 2 July 1574
> (Clwyd Record Office, D/NH/822)

A verbose **bargain and sale** with feoffment and endorsement of livery of seisin was usual until around 1680. The operative words were 'aliened granted bargained sold enfeoffed and confirmed'.

The secret conveyance yet triumphed, through the cunning of lawyers, with two documents (one folded in the other) known as **lease and release** referring to leasehold interests created out of the freehold (which need not be enrolled). The process received court sanction in 1621. On one day A bargained and sold a lease of a tenement to B for one year at a nominal consideration. A was seised to the use of B. The legal estate vested in B without livery or enrolment. A retained his reversion which, as an incorporeal hereditament (right pertaining to the property), he released next day by deed without livery to B (already in possession) for a substantial consideration. The operative words were 'have granted aliened released and confirmed'. The lease and release were the usual conveyancing documents (widely employed also to create passive trusts to effect settlements) until replaced by a statutory release in 1841 and deed of grant in 1845.

An estate in fee tail was an interest carved out of an estate in fee simple, limited to the heirs of the grantee's body and, upon failure, reverting (generally) to the grantor or his heirs or to remaindermen. Following a statute of 1285 an entailed estate could not be alienated by a tenant in tail beyond his lifetime and was thus inalienable for as long as the family line endured. **Entails** tended to conflict with sound estate management and were against the policy of the law regarding free alienation. Thus legislation of 1535 provided that a conveyance to feoffees to uses created a fee simple rather than limited estate. In partial compensation for the loss of the use, two-thirds of a man's property could from 1540 be devised and limited by will (which became for the first time evidence of title). Chancery stepped in during the seventeenth century to permit trusts and settlements, perhaps on marriage. Thus X covenanted with Y to stand seised to the use of X for life then to the use of X's son Z and Z's wife, daughter of Y. The entail became a popular means of safeguarding the integrity of estates and (until 1878) a married woman's rights to her own property. The circumvention of entails taxed the ingenuity of lawyers, who waxed fat on the proceeds of legal cases. Entails could be barred by fine or recovery until 1833, thereafter by a disentailing deed enrolled in chancery.

Customary tenures unrecognised at common law were created by feudal lords for their tenants. Transactions were recorded in baron court records (now held by the lord of the manor, record office or library) with copies extracted as title deeds for the relevant copyholders (still held among the title deeds to the descendant tenement). Inheritance customs varied (inheritance by primogeniture; or 'borough English' to the youngest son; or for lives; or equally among the sons, known in Kent as 'gavelkind'). **Copyhold** was altered to common-law tenure by a deed of enfranchisement. A new grant by the lord was indicated by the words *ad hanc curiam venit X ... et cepit de domino ... tenementum* ('X came to this court and took the tenement from the lord'). A tenement changed hands in a deed of surrender (by the vendor into the lord's hands) and admittance (of the purchaser on payment of a fine). A copyholder could surrender his tenement for readmittance subject to the uses of a deed of mortgage or a will. He could even suffer a recovery.

12. The naming of houses

House names appear in documents and plans, in faded signs printed on the ginnels and twittens of the town, and in the memories of local folk. The names of house and neighbourhood suggest aspects of history, though caution is required in interpretation. Spurious medievalisms (Monkhall, Castlefield) attach to modern properties; a new name (Laburnum Lodge) to a medieval manor house. A name with significance and history (Wood Farm) may be displaced by a stylishly euphonious but insignificant name (Waystrode Manor): Abbot's Fireside, the modern name of a fifteenth-century house at Elham, Kent, was previously successively known as Smithies Arms and Keeler's Mansions. Names may be corrupt but significant derivations, for instance, Bag o' Nails from the Badger's Nale (the hawker's alehouse). In Celtic lands names written down by anglicised occupiers are particularly difficult to interpret (Cluoneogullane, Uregarehill alias Ffarrenhenryroe). New names for new houses reflect the tastes of the times and battles long ago. Villas named Dunrobin, Balmoral and Lochnagar are redolent of Victorian romanticism. Houses named Alma, Sebastopol and Balaclava celebrate the Crimean War (1854-6).

Linguistic elements in house names indicate former incarnations of building or site. Celtic elements suggesting 'dwelling' include Scottish Gaelic *baile* (*baile na gobhainn*, 'house of the blacksmith') and *clachan*, 'stone house'; Cornish *lis*, 'lord's hall'; Irish *teamhair*, 'hilltop residence' (anglicised as Tara); Welsh *tref*, 'homestead'. Grander fortifications may incorporate Welsh *caer*, 'stockaded homestead'; Old British *dūnos*, 'fort' (*dinas* in Welsh); Irish *ráth*, 'defended farmhouse'.

The names of homesteads named or renamed by English settlers from the fifth century onwards might contain the elements *cot*, *aern*, *bōtl* and *hām* (Thatcham, *thaec-hām*, 'thatched homestead'). The element *tūn* denoted originally 'stockaded site' but could be attached to the principal house of a manor established by English lords from the ninth century onwards (Knighton, *cniht-tūn*, 'retainer's farmstead'). The elements *stead*, *stow* and *stock*, 'place', were attached to religious sites as well as homesteads and farmsteads. *Stock* particularly denoted an outlying farm. *Wick*, 'dwelling', implied special agricultural or trading connections (cheese, salt, wool, grain).

The Danish elements *bý*, *thorp* and *toft* denoted 'homestead', though later 'village'. The Norse *thveit* indicates a forest clearing or moorland enclosure where a settler made his home (Robiewhat, 'Hrothbiartr's clearing/paddock'). A Norse element for a dwelling, *bolstathr*, was shortened in place-names as *-bister* or *-bost*. The element *buth*, originally a mere shelter, was at first applied to temporary fortified camps established by raiders and later to the principal house of the local warlord. *Skáli* also denoted a manorial residence from the tenth century in the forms *scale*, *shiel* or *skaill*. The element *quoy* was attached to Norse farmsteads founded on marginal higher ground, probably during the tenth and eleventh centuries.

A house name may recall wild creatures of the vicinity: Boarzell, 'boar'; Wolvey, 'enclosure to protect flocks from wolves'; or farm animals: Mochdre (Welsh), 'pig farm'; Shipdham, 'homestead with sheep cote'. Crops are recalled in Haydock (Welsh), 'barley farm', and in Flaxhouse.

Industry and trade are evidenced in houses with such elements as the Gaelic-derived *gow*, 'smith', the English *bleach*, *mill*, *furnace*, *shambles*, *cordiner*, *tanyard*; and the Welsh *felin* or *melin*, 'mill', *pandy*, 'fulling mill'. Bridford View recalls a river crossing, Ferriby House a ferry, Toll Cottage a turnpike gate. Inn names refer to a local landowner (Bristol Arms), hero (York Tavern), principal class of patron (Navigation Inn) or legendary figure (Green Man). Names were periodically altered (Red Lion giving way to Hero of Waterloo in 1815). Essex Street, Dublin, was named for the Earl of Essex, Lord Lieutenant 1672-7; the Elephant Inn there was named for an elephant exhibited on the site, killed in a fire on 17th June 1681 and dissected in the interests of science.

Manorial or **demesne** origin may be inferred from the English elements *barton*, *town*, *great*, *mains*, *hall*, *court*, and the Welsh *plas*, *t) mawr*; **ecclesiastical** connections from Latin loan-words such as *díseart*, 'hermitage', *mynach*, 'monk', *eccles*, *kil*, 'cell, church', from Old British *landa*, 'church', and from the self-explanatory modern English elements *grange*, *nun*, *monk*, *abbey*; political or **administrative** history from English *thing*, *moot*, *bury*, *shire*, *hundred*, *vestry*, *town* elements (Hungercut Hall, Suffolk, was the courthouse for the hundred).

A house may be named for an owner or occupier, past or present. Slippery Sam's restaurant, Petham, Kent, recalls an eighteenth-century smuggler who occupied what was then Stone Street farmhouse. The house name may recall an occupier's home town, residence or workplace (Kandy, Cathay, Montrose).

13. The family home

The family papers of generations of people who have owned, occupied and visited a house grant a privileged glimpse of the domestic trivia and intimacies which haunt every household. Papers may be deposited for safe keeping in the archives at the public library or county record office though more usually remain in the family's possession, enshrined in opulent albums, neglected in a corner of an attic or lodged with a local lawyer.

Account books, bills and voucher bundles record a family's expenditure on household necessities, major repairs and renovations. Houses are discussed in letters and diaries. The **memoirs** of the travelling preacher James Allan (1670-1740) preserve an unexcelled picture of domestic life in the province of Moray. The memoirs describe lodgings in a typical hall-and-chamber house on the Black Isle:

> just over the ferie wher I lodged in one Elphingstoun ane innkeeper his house ... But ye chamber filled so with smoak yt I was forced to come & sit down with these in the house ... That night because of ye smoak I had opened the window in ye chamber & forgetting to close it, was much the worse of ye air, it being just opposit to my bed ... my cheek began to swell, & yr began ane ulcer upon it

The memoirs set out the date and reasons for the building of Allan's own house at Echt, Aberdeenshire:

> ... fearing that my going away would be a heavier burthen to the Lady [Echt] then she could get born for she could never hear of it & for hindring of me had got a litle house erected for me & was provideing & putting into it all necessaries.
> (Elgin Public Library DBL 79/1, 8th November 1689, June 1690.)

Every family accumulates **albums** of photographs of house and home and a clutter of **printed ephemera** which assist an imaginative reconstruction of an earlier age: handbills advertising the sale by auction of a bankrupt household; samples of wallpaper, oilcloth and curtaining; catalogues for the newest lines in water closets, gas cookers, coppers, mangles and foldaway baths.

14. Estate houses

Estate muniments chart the histories of houses erected on lands owned by church, state, nobility, National Trust, gentry, industry, financial institution, *et cetera*. Estate owners were responsible for capitalist's villa, terraced (or garden city) barracking for workers, speculative suburbia, gentleman's seat, tacksman's house, tenant's farmstead, crofter's cottage, labourer's hall and farmservant's bothy. Estate muniments, if not deposited in library or record office, must be sought at the company head office, at the estate office or with the lawyer who acted as agent, factor or secretary.

A panoply of **legal** documents — title deeds, marriage contracts, jointures, agreements, processes — concern the ownership, settlement, inheritance and tenancy of manor house, dower house, lodges and cottages. The cost of building and restoration may be determined from cash books, ledgers and voucher files.

The farming **lease** emerged at the end of the twelfth century. Leases (tacks in Scotland) for years or lives were required in writing in Scots law from 1449 and in England from 1677. Indeed, unwritten understandings between landowner and peasant remained normal until the eighteenth century — the illiteracy of the tenantry and the absence of writings conspiring to ease the processes of clearance and enclosure. The operative words were 'demise grant and to farm let', followed by the 'habendum' defining the term (one life, three lives, seven, 21, 99 years, *et cetera)* and the 'reddendum' stating rent and services ('1s 4d, a fat hen at Christmas, £2 10s heriot'). A fine might also be demanded. Cancelled leases were rarely preserved, being unnecessary as evidence of title. Leases could be assigned to third parties, particularly to creditors, lawyers or bankers. On 16th November 1698 Edward Salusbury, a landed gentleman of Galltvaenan, Denbighshire, assigned for £10 to Richard Cumberland, citizen and stationer of London, his interest in a lease of Ann Moseley's valuable messuage new built on the south-east corner of Cannon alias Pissing Alley in the London parish of St Gregory (Clwyd Record Office D/GA/728).

Rents might be paid in cash, though until the eighteenth century payment in kind was more suited to the economy of unimproved peasant husbandry. The **rental** due from 'Alexr. Mathew on the south side of the Burn' on the lands of Lieutenant John Rose, principal tacksman of Cloves, Moray, in 1773 was three bolls (a measure of capacity, eventually fixed at 6 imperial bushels) victual, £3 13s 3d sterling money, three poultry (worth 2d each), one hen (worth 6d), one day's labour at lint work (linen making) at 6d, and two hooks (reapers to cut the laird's corn at harvest time) at 6d each (J. R. Barrett, Elgin, 2/19).

Leases of property were employed as security for money loans from the twelfth century. The demise specified a long term (five hundred years or more), cancelled on repayment of principal and interest. The key words followed the 'reddendum': 'provided always and upon condition ... shall well and truly pay'. Certain types of pledges may be difficult to recognise as **mortgages**, for instance those effected by feoffment with livery of seisin or by lease and release without 'reddendum' or 'proviso'. Mortgage documents of the nineteenth century may include a block plan, plans of each floor of a house (with valuable fireplaces, boilers, sinks, bath and water closet), elevations to show bay windows, back kitchens, roofing, chimneys and decorative finials — all of which might otherwise be plundered. Mortgages facilitated the raising of money for house purchase, alteration or construction and could be assigned to third parties. From 1677 the assignment of a term in trust to attend the freehold and inheritance was employed to dispose of a tenement and redeem the mortgage simultaneously.

A house was appraised at the conclusion of a tenant's term:

> birly men to the Laird of Graingehill ... vieued ... the Fyre-house possest by Peter Martine in Boigs removeing tenent Now entring to be posest by James Hendry ... They Compryse ... the s[ai]d fyre house ... Consisting of One Couple and tuelve sides With the Door and Door Cheeks ... To Seven Merks Scots Mony.
> (J. R. Barrett, Elgin, 4/3, 15th May 1729.)

Valuators described accommodation and fittings:

> The little wardrop tuo glass windous whole except tuo lossens with Lock & Key
> The heigh east roume
> The midroum & Closset
> The wester big roum tuo sash windous
> The Dining roum ... Door wt a snake
> (J. R. Barrett, Elgin, 4/3, Moy house, 1724.)

A word-picture (**survey**) of a property was particularly popular from about 1540 to 1780:

> One litle house adioyning unto the Churcheyard ... newly reedified consisteth in these roomes followinge viz a hall, a kitchen & a buttery roome upon the first storye & three lodginge roomes over them upon the seconde storye & a seller vaulted under the buttery, And this house as it seemeth hath bene newelye repayred to the intente to

make it a dwellinge house for the mynister theare.
(Hatfield House Library, Cecil family papers, General 41/7, 1606.)

Estate **maps and plans** showing individual tenements and houses, annotated with rentals, acreages, place-names, occupiers' names, *et cetera,* became usual from around 1740 as enclosure and agrarian change gathered pace. During the eighteenth century towns and cities broke their medieval bounds: urban landlords and speculative developers mapped the spread of building across their suburban estates.

And when, at last, a landed family decayed and the estate was sold, an opulent printed **catalogue** (illustrated with maps, plans and pictures) described every parcel of land, house, mill, byre and dovecote — emphasising in fulsome agent's jargon the chief selling points of each, glossing over the dilapidations of penury and long decline.

The proprietor of a medieval landed estate (lord of the manor, barony, bailiary or regality) governed his domain through a **manor court**. The court noted depredations and dilapidations which diminished the value of the patrimony. Court proceedings recorded the lord's attention to his property, enforcing dues and customs and deciding disputes over tenure:

> John Sanders ... depones that [James Grant] & his predecessors were in use to occupy & possess the House lybelled ever since he minds & that the Ridge goes immediatly up by the Gavel of the House, & that he does not know whether it be a part of the common Muir or Croft ... The Bailie ... finds the said James Grant has right to the ... House ... [but] shall not subset ... but allenarly during the Markets held yearly on the hill of Kieth.
> (Moray District Record Office, ZVOg B2/20, regality of Ogilvie, 12th and 17th July 1744.)

15. Business

Business records narrate the history of a house from a variety of angles: as a product (of a building firm); as investment; as insurance risk; as home for worker or manager; as commercial or industrial premises. A sample of local business records may be lodged (after weeding) in record office or library; more extensive collections must be sought in solicitors' collections and company offices.

Houses may be referred to in company prospectus or minute book, in correspondence file and letter book. Legal files mention houses: in disputes with adjacent proprietors, in agreements for the supply of goods and services, in suits over pollution and nuisance. The building, renting, renovation or alteration of a house will be identified, costed and dated in financial records of a relevant firm (day book, cash book, ledger, voucher). All businesses accumulate fat files of ephemera: brochures, maps, photographs, handbills, catalogues and advertising material relating to associated or client housing. Plans of industrial premises (mill, factory, workshop) and commercial emporia (counting house, warehouse, hotel, shop), variously converted from and into houses, are preserved in the company archives.

Insurance companies flourished from the seventeenth century onwards, insuring business premises and private houses against fire, flood and other risks. Each house was identified by a tin or lead badge affixed to the façade showing a company logo and, perhaps, a policy number (referring to company registers). Registers held by company head offices and local agents (policies remained in the hands or deed bundles of householders) recorded the name, calling and abode of the holder with descriptions and perhaps plans of property insured, particularly detailed from around 1840 onwards. Records may be lodged in local record offices, though the most extensive collections are in the Guildhall Library, London (indexes published on microfiche).

Architectural practices were founded throughout the British Isles during the eighteenth century, and archives may be preserved from that period, held perhaps by a successor architectural firm, by a county record office or library, a university library, one of the three Royal Commissions on Historical Monuments, or the British Architectural Library (drawings collection), 21 Portman Square, London W1 (Royal Institute of British Architects). The archives of architects and land surveyors include architectural drawings (plan, elevation, section, perspective). Specifications, contracts and correspondence refer to the original conception and subsequent remodellings of a house. The documents show external appearance at various dates, internal accommodation, fixtures, fittings and amenities (water closet, presses, ventilation, heating, lighting, bathroom, laundry, cesspit, ashpit, cellarage, drains):

> Carpenter Work
> the sashes shall be $2^3/8$ inch thick ... Drawing room Dining Room Ante room and Library shall be glased with $1/4$ inch thick British plate glass ... Dados Soffits & sides shall be of framed panneled and moulded work to match the doors ... The seats in the outer Water closets shall be of inch dressed deal with framed parts of the same and lids hinged with brass hinges and all fitted up with skirting 7 inches deep, to have a cistern capable of containing 30 cubic feet of water ... well supported.
> (J. W. Wittet, architects, Elgin, Logie House, 1861.)

The province of Moray was blessed with talented architects (collections now in Moray District Record Office). William Robertson (1786-1841), succeeded by his nephews A. and W. Reid and by J. and W. Wittet, Elgin, designed houses throughout the region. The calendar of his drawings demonstrates the development of his ideas as a leader of the baronial revival and permits the researcher to date with some confidence undocumented houses in the distinctive 'Robertson style'. The archive of the architect Charles C. Doig (1855-1918) — thirty thousand plans and one hundred thousand working papers — documents one man's work: mundane houses for local authorities; smart villas for private individuals; surveys of estates and farms; humble sheds, farm buildings and sties. Doig's fortuitous location in rural Scotland during the whisky boom and his constructional inventiveness made his name as an architect of distilleries and their villages (houses for workers, managers, gaugers) from Kirkwall to Islay.

Estate agents and auctioneers accumulated unequalled documentation on houses (with fulsome descriptions), their contents and occupants, though some little imagination is required to recreate a household from an auctioneer's handbill advertising a sale or a valuation of a bankrupt's sequestrated assets. Notices and particulars of sale with plans, photographs and correspondence files form extensive archives in agency offices (comparatively few collections having been deposited in record offices or libaries).

4. EASTER GLACKTON.
The Dwelling-House contains Parlour, three Bed-Rooms, Kitchen, Milk-House, Coal-House, &c. The Steading of Offices consist of Stable ... Byres ... Loose Box, Courts for twenty Cattle, Tool-House, Men's Apartment, Barn, Granary, &c.

6.   WOODSIDE CROFT.
The Cottage consists of Room, Kitchen, &c.

7.   SCHOOL CROFT.
The Dwelling-House is comfortable, substantial and in good order.
It contains Room, Closet, Kitchen, &c.
(J. R. Barrett, Elgin, 1/5, particulars of sale, Gollanfield, Inverness-
shire, June 1874.)

A law practice accumulates papers of thousands of clients, including deeds, plans, files and surveys of their houses. The firm's
own archive (volumes of indexed in-letters, out-letters and legal
drafts) documents a client's house chronologically, though inter-
spersed with the business of other clients (and thus usually restricted for a period of one hundred years). Ledgers supply an
index to the solicitors' clients and concerns as secretary to local
firms, as agent to insurance companies, and as confidential adviser
to local folk enmeshed in bankruptcies, neighbourly disputes, di-
vorce settlements, marriage contracts and house purchase. Mil-
lions of clients' bundles from lawyers' offices have been deposited
in record offices (notably through the efforts in London of the
British Records Association) but law firms' own archives are rare:
an exceptional provincial exemplar is that of J. and H. W. Leask,
solicitors, of Forres, some three thousand volumes deposited in
1976.

Turnpike trusts, established by act of Parliament to build or re-
pair roads and bridges, financed operations with tolls farmed out to
contractors. From a bay-fronted cottage breasting the highway, the
tollkeeper watched his stretch of road, diligently collecting his fee
before turning open the gate to traffic. Turnpike houses have generally been converted into comfortable modern homes. Minutes,
accounts and plans should be incorporated in county archives at the
record office:

> Toll-houses ... ought to be of that description of cottages called
> 'stake and rise' about twenty seven feet long by twelve within
> walls, properly lighted and thatched, and which ... are both cheap
> and durable.
> (Moray Record Office, ZCMm RT2/1, Elginshire, 30th April
> 1811.)

Schools, hospitals, orphanages and free dispensaries were generally private or charitable enterprises before the twentieth century.
Operations were not infrequently accommodated in ordinary houses.
Thus a researcher may be dismayed to discover from institutional
minutes held by local solicitors that his home, just outside the

borough boundary, was appropriated for a cholera hospital in the 1830s or that his secluded villa served as an asylum. An endowed foundation required purpose-built accommodation: neat terraces of cottaging for beadsmen, decayed craftsmen or disabled war veterans; an edifice of polite architecture to represent the worthy ideals of educational and medical institutions. Teachers' houses or porters' lodges remain as homes long after institutions are closed, demolished or converted to other (perhaps domestic) use.

Superintendent's House, Papplewick Pumping Station, Nottinghamshire. In 1884 the Nottingham waterworks were improved with the erection of a lavish pumping station (by the Nottingham civil engineer Marriott Ogle Tarbolton; beam engines by James Watt and Company) at Papplewick. A commodious house was erected for the works. The clients favoured an Arts and Crafts style and the architect contrived each elevation of the house to delight the viewer with a different aspect of mock-timbered gables, sweeping eaves, broad verges and bay windows. Simple vernacular materials (brick, stone, tile, wood) are imaginatively combined to create features of interest such as the fancy-headed windows divided by mullions and transoms, and the jaunty brick chimney stack with its spiky pots. (Photograph: Cadbury Lamb.)

16. Quarter sessions

Justices of the peace convened in judicial and administrative sessions from the fourteenth century onwards. These 'godlie wyse and vertuous', but amateur, gentlemen were assisted on the bench by a local lawyer who, as clerk of the peace, advised on points of law, prepared calendars of cases and preserved session rolls. Records are normally held in local record offices (or the Scottish Record Office and National Library of Wales).

The justices met as a formal court four times a year (quarter sessions) though, between times, an individual magistrate might dispense summary justice in his own parlour (petty session). Session records preserve a priceless fund of information on local folk and incidentally on the homes in which they lived and worked — or the houses which they burgled.

The justices were responsible for a variety of county property, and records may reveal the earlier history of a house as asylum, hospital, bridewell, jail or keeper's cottage.

Administrative duties expanded during the sixteenth century as the justices listed, licensed, supervised, assessed and taxed people and property throughout the shire. Deeds of bargain and sale were enrolled from 1536. From 1552 the clerk recorded recognisances of good behaviour on behalf of licensed victuallers, while bonds issued by licensing magistrates were preserved from 1780 to 1828. Registers of applications and licences show a remarkable number of homes at some time in the past functioning as beershop or public house, perhaps the small business of an enterprising widow if not a front for a fence or a brothel. Between 1662 and 1689 hearth tax was assessed: village constables served as chimneymen, lodging lists of taxable and exempt householders and their hearths. Houses erected for and used by religious dissenters were registered from 1689 to 1852 (papists registered from 1791). Land-tax assessments from 1692 onwards were registered (as an electoral qualification 1780-1832), recording taxable properties (including houses, factories, mills, *et cetera*), their owners and occupiers. Window tax was collected 1696-1851: returns showing names, residence and number of windows may indicate when (but not why) patterns of fenestration were created (or bricked up). Houses in the vicinity of road diversions and closures were documented from 1697 (plans from 1773). Following the Jacobite rising of 1715 papists were obliged to register their names and descriptions of their properties and, as a further check on dissent, were required (from 1717) to enroll their wills and title deeds. Enclosure of common fields, moor, waste and village green was facilitated from around 1760 by private acts of Parliament and by general enclosure acts of 1801-45: awards, agreements and plans were drawn up — showing before and after housescapes — and deposited with the clerk of the peace. From 1786 the clerk collected information concerning parochial charities (and memorials concerning their property from 1812), preliminary to making returns to government. Electoral lists, detailing name, residence, calling and place of qualification of voters, were deposited following reform of the franchise in 1832. Session records include deposited books of reference and documentation accompanying plans showing housing in the vicinity of canals (from 1792) and subsequently of railways, harbours, waterworks and other public undertakings. Barges and bargees on inland waterways were registered from 1795 to 1871 — a priceless source for the houseboat community.

St Ronan's, Forres, Moray, Grampian. In November 1875 Dr William Loch Stuart of Bothwell purchased 'a croft of four ridges ... a field of land ... and two roods ... in the Nether Crofts of Forres ... extending from the public road to the old run of the burn of Mossat ... together with a villa or Dwelling House erected thereon.' To buy this comfortable, newly completed, centrally heated dream house Dr Stuart was obliged to borrow £1000 (at 5 per cent per annum interest). A large conservatory added to the side of the house accommodated the doctor's passion for palms and ferns. The name chosen for the house has no local significance: the several saints named Ronan were active in south Scotland and in Ireland. The name perhaps suggests that Dr Stuart's taste in literature included Sir Walter Scott's popular novel 'St Ronan's Well'. Surprisingly perhaps, this is not a 'listed building'. (Photograph: David Iredale)

17. Local government

Local government archives (borough, county, commissioners of supply, grand jury, *et cetera*) are deposited in libraries and record offices or retained by officials.

Local authorities framed byelaws to regulate buildings: 'for preventing fire ... no house shall be thatched with heather' (Elgin, 1747). Minute books enshrined council decisions:

> John Smith anent his Residing with his Family at Lossiemouth ... in the Townhouse ... to Keep intertainment for Strangers and to do such other services in assisting Sailors ... and what further may be in his power for the service & Good of the Harbour and Community.
> (Moray District Record Office, ZBEL A2/13, Elgin, 14th March 1748.)

Petitions from individuals and groups of citizens sought redress of grievances, removal of nuisances and official assistance, while noticing for posterity petitioners' addresses and houses causing offence:

> John Shanks Keeper of the Gate of the Elgin Cathedral ... lives on the north side ... on the south side are two establishments for the gratification of the carnal passions — That are frequently attended, and as often has your petitioner been aroused ...
> (Moray District Record Office, ZBE1 A3/835/6, Elgin Town Council, 1835.)

A variety of courts considered tenancies, debts, bankruptcies, rents and boundaries. Dean of guild courts were specially concerned with neighbourhood disputes arising from common gables, overhanging eaves, encroachments and nuisances. The dean supervised renovation of ruinous houses — 'the Eastmost fore-house and fore-stair ... with the upper loft above the same, together with the two fore-booths or Shops under' (Elgin, 1791) — preserving tradesmen's bills in official files:

> To 2 Dozen Flooring Deals for a Room in the House [of John Duncan, merchant] @ 7s
> To 4 hundred nails for do @ 7d
> To Mending the Plaister of 2 Rooms & a Stair Case and Whitewashing the same 2s
> To Wood and workemanship putting in a Beam to Support the Garret Floor 5s
> (Moray District Record Office, ZBE1 D3/791/1 and 789/1/6 Elgin, 1791 and 1789.)

Extensive collections of architectural plans were deposited under public health, building and planning regulations, forming an archive of almost every house altered or erected from the nineteenth century onwards. The local authority also preserved plans of its own properties.

Title deeds to council housing (including beadhouse, workhouse, schoolhouse, mayor's mansion) are supported by leases and agreements narrating long legal histories of former uses and previous occupants. Tenders, specifications and contract files document the erection of municipal properties:

> Eight [houses] each ... 30 feet Long ... 13 feet wide ... Seven feet high ... two windows half wood half Glass in each ... walls to be harled with Lime ... the whole ... to be built with Clay. The Inside to be Plaistred with Clay ... Thatched with Divots and Clay & Straw ... to have thirteen Coples Sawen out of 24 feet Spars of Abernethy wood ... each house a Timber Lumb ... £90 Sterling
> (Moray District Record Office, ZBE1 A37/3/21, Lossiemouth, 1784.)

Boroughs and counties registered property in response to administrative necessity and legal obligation. New buildings and alterations of existing structures were regulated from the foundation of the borough, though building control registers and minutes with files of applications, warrants, correspondence and plans rarely date from earlier than the eighteenth century (planning records only from 1944 and certain county districts as late as 1954). Shops, workshops, dairies, unfit houses and common lodging houses were registered and recorded:

> Common Lodging-Houses
> House in Hays Close 86, High Street Elgin occupied by Elizabeth McBean or McGillivray
> This House consists of two Rooms and a kitchen and small Closet which has hitherto been used as a Bed Room for two Persons although it only contains accommodation for one.
> This woman's Husband is seldom at home ...
> Rooms are as follows viz:-
> No. 1 1200 Cubic feet of Space & capable of Accommodating four Persons ...
> (Moray District Record Office, ZBE1 F77/869/2, Elgin Police Commission, 1869.)

Council housing was registered under acts of 1919 onwards, subsidised houses for rural workers from 1926. Registers maintained by the inspector of the poor report on the domestic circumstances of paupers relieved in their own homes.

From the fourteenth century onwards in certain incorporated towns valuations, assessments, rate books and cess and stent rolls (assessments for taxation) referred to individual houses by district, street, name and numbers, showing annual rates due from named owners and occupiers according to property value and extent. Valuations for rural areas date chiefly from reforms of 1744. Irish valuation was reformed in 1826-52, Scottish in 1855. Cash books, ledgers and vouchers balance income from rents and rates against expenditure on council property (farmhouse, workhouse, teacher's house), including house construction and property maintenance.

Official correspondence in files and letterbooks referred to the domestic concerns of borough, parish, town and county. Houses (overcrowded, insanitary, dilapidated) were inspected and measured for the purpose of action (demolition, sale, *et cetera*) or for reports to central government:

> Housing (inspection of district) Regulations (Scotland) 1928.
> 45, High Street ... walls are of stone, plastered on the hard and partly wood lined ... roof is heavy slated and is done ... general dampness Gas Lighting ... wc ... common to 7 tenants; the water is laid on to a sink at the stair landing ... used by 2 tenants
> (Moray District Record Office, ZBE1 E46/1/290, Elgin, 1934.)

Beach House, Sidmouth, Devon. Sidmouth, a prosperous medieval seaport, declined when its harbour silted up, but it revived as a holiday resort from the early nineteenth century when sea bathing became popular. The Beach House (about 1820) shows a typical Regency façade, with gothick fenestration, bright white stucco and a delicate wrought-iron balcony with a tent-like canopy. The style, typical of the early nineteenth-century resort, is to be found elsewhere in England, most notably at Brighton. (Photograph: David Iredale.)

18. The public records

Records of national government departments are lodged in the Public Record Offices in Belfast, Dublin, Edinburgh and London and in the National Library of Wales at Aberystwyth.

Exchequer originated during the twelfth century as the financial department of government. Collections of the crown's feudal revenue created records of houses, mills, manors and tenements such as the county surveys known as hundred rolls of 1275-6 and *quo waranto* pleas from 1278. Hearth-tax returns for England and Wales, 1662-89 (Scotland, 1691, 1694), are among useful records concerning houses. Property on crown estates was closely documented, particularly from the sixteenth century, when monastic and chantry assets were absorbed. Buildings (and accompanying records) sequestrated for Parliament after 1643 were described in detail before lease or sale. Popish recusant and Jacobite estates were registered or annexed after the rebellions of 1715 and 1745. In Ireland redistribution of property during the seventeenth century created Strafford's inquisitions on property (1633-40), civil survey from 1654, William Petty's down survey (parish and barony maps) 1655-6, and books of survey and distribution from 1662.

Treasury archives include house duties in London, 1698-1778; land taxes, 1799-1963; parochial tax ledgers from 1864 (London from 1857) to 1937; a land tax domesday for various years between 1798 and 1914; and window, house, shop, *et cetera*, taxation (in Scotland) variously, 1747-1812. The national survey of land-ownership under the Finance Act 1909-10, compiled throughout Britain and Ireland, dealt with every discrete holding or house.

Chancery in its administrative capacity enrolled court decrees and title deeds concerning houses, for example charity, chapel, family and estate property on the dorse (back) of the close rolls from the fourteenth century. Inquisitions *post mortem* (to 1660), following the death of a tenant in chief, valued houses, mills, manors, charities, *et cetera,* with a view to maximising Crown revenue. Inquisitions from 1516 investigated the decay of hamlets and houses since 1488 through clearances for sheep. The service of heirs in Scotland concerned the succession to heritable property (including specified houses) from 1545.

Records of the **Privy Council** and its committees (Star Chamber, requests, trade, education) refer to property of the rich and famous as well as poor men's houses, buildings of industry and commerce, schoolhouses, *et cetera*. State papers from the sixteenth century onwards on home affairs (law, order, agriculture, industry, military, education, paupers, religion, *et cetera*) include reports, correspondence and plans on relevant housing.

Housing figured significantly in the deliberations of government agencies for economic development, for instance the Board of Manufactures in Scotland, 1727-1927. The Forestry Commission (1919) accumulated archives of ancient forests and foresters' houses, for example in the Forest of Dean's industrial hamlets from 1662. Nationalised industries inherited business and estate muniments of predecessor companies (colliery, shipyard, canal, harbour, railway, gas, steel, *et cetera*). Rentals, plans, correspondence and reports on housing belonging to the company or in the vicinity of company installations may be held in local and national record offices or in the industry's own record centre.

Housing figured largely in records of the government's intervention or supervision over local authorities in matters of poor relief, public health, sewerage, planning, water supply, *et cetera*, in the archives of the Ministries of Housing, Local Government, Health, Agriculture, *et cetera*. The government facilitated the sale of incumbered estates in Ireland from 1849 through commissioners whose court rentals and maps particularised houses, shops and farms. New houses were established through the Irish Land Commission (1881) and Congested Districts Board (1891-1923). Royal commissions, public inquiries and judicial inquiries informed public opinion on matters of public moment such as housing.

The Valuation Office Survey of Ireland was initiated in 1809. Surveyors drew up large-scale town plans. House books contained the dimension, quality and value of each dwelling:

> Revd. Mr Stewart Muff Lodge: House Basement Story Stable Offices Open Sheds & privy ... a nice situation. a good distance from the road. Small yard well enclosed
> (Public Record Office of Ireland, OL 5.0817, survey and house book, Innishowen W barony, County Donegal, 17th April 1839.)

Records of tenure books name owners, occupiers and immediate lessors of houses, with notes on tenure and year of last letting.

Legal cases involving property were heard in various national courts of law. King's Bench (from 1194) heard questions affecting the king's peace such as theft and trespass as well as personal actions of ejectment (titles to freehold property). Common Pleas heard civil disputes as well as fines and recoveries (to establish title). Exchequer dealt with financial problems (tithe, debt to Crown) and ejectment. In Scotland the central civil and criminal Court of Session derived from medieval institutions: processes survive from 1527. The Scottish Land Court for crofting properties commenced work in 1886. Chancery was notionally a poor man's court, protecting property rights. In the Court of Bankruptcy (records 1710-1873) estates and dwellings were specified in particular detail. Itinerant justices were dispatched by medieval kings to determine cases of rape, riot, robbery, *et cetera*. The assize system developed in England during the thirteenth century (Scottish ayre records only from 1493). In Wales the Court of Great Sessions was founded in 1543. Courts, established in the shires from the twelfth century, heard such cases as disputes among householders, theft from property, arson, removal of tenants (including the notorious highland clearances).

South Moreton, Oxfordshire. This 'olde worlde' thatched cottage represents the home of a small farmer. The house (like most old houses) is evidently of several builds. The house is of box-frame construction, but of relatively slight timbers, suggesting a date late in the timber-framed era. The right-hand bay is jettied in the common form of a two-storeyed end and is perhaps a survival from an earlier single-ended (hall and solar) structure. The central bay is of late seventeenth-century date (with more recent windows). The brick chimney was added vernacularly exterior to the timber frame but has been incorporated subsequently within a separately roofed bay. Modern expectations (of separate kitchen and bathroom facilities) have required further extension. This is also in timber, but not in the true tradition, and, atypically for this area, weatherboarded. (Photograph: Raymond Lea.)

19. Ecclesiastical sources

Ecclesiastical archives demonstrate the dutiful care of the church for its real and spiritual estate. Records of the Church of England (if not retained in the appropriate cathedral or church) are located to designated local record offices. Provincial (archbishopric) records are at Lambeth Palace (for Canterbury) and the Borthwick Institute of Historical Research (for York), though Prerogative Court of Canterbury wills have been deposited in the Public Record Office. Estate muniments of the Church of England are held in the Church Commission's record office at 1 Millbank, London SW1. Nonconformist records may be centralised (for example Methodist archives at John Rylands University Library of Manchester), though the majority remain in the custody of local lawyers, church officials, record offices and libraries. Welsh church and probate records before 1858 are largely at the National Library of Wales. Scottish Kirk Session, presbytery, synod, General Assembly and commissary (probate) records are usually located through the Scottish Record Office. Archives of the Church of Ireland, including the representative church body (trustees of property), are being collected in the library at Braemor Park, Rathgar, Dublin 14. Probate records before 1900 were destroyed in 1922.

Capitular archives document the deliberations of the Dean and Chapter governing a cathedral or free chapel: maintaining fabric, administering almshouses and hospitals, managing estates and overseeing property leased for residential or industrial purposes.

Provincial records (of the Archbishops of Canterbury and York) comprise minutes, court books, act books, correspondence and petitions depicting the moral state of congregations and the structural condition of churches and miscellaneous property.

Diocesan clerks maintained, from the thirteenth century, registers, journals and account books whose content ranged across the bishop's broad responsibilities for his see, its people and property. In his courts the bishop determined property disputes and delivered verdicts on fornication, plunder and adultery — intriguing glimpses of goings-on behind a godly façade. He registered the houses in which dissenters were permitted to worship under the Toleration Act of 1688. He required answers to queries (on charities, houses, granges, *et cetera*) before personal visitations of parishes:

> a very ancient House yet calld Abbot Hall; also a very remarkable Well [site of pagan ritual and Celtic hermitage] ... with a little House adjoyning called the Anchorage.
> (Cheshire Record Office, EDA/6/7/96, Well and Snape, 26th April 1722).

Visitation findings might be collated as a comprehensive survey (*speculum*) of the diocese — a parish by parish inventory of assets, incomes, properties and privileges.

> Sr Edward Coddington Knt did hold 6 Townes ... to pay 5 li for a Herriott to build 2 English houses upon ye lands and one fayre stone house wth in ye Citty to find 2 light horses for his Maties Service
> (Trinity College Library, Dublin, MS 865 (formerly F.1.22), survey of the temporalities of the Archbishropic of Armagh, about 1622.)

Under canons of 1571 and 1604 (and especially after 1660) church property was inventoried in documents known as **terriers**:

> a Four square brick house three stories high besides cellars containing four rooms in each story with a closet in the two first stories — an outhouse of two bays of building one used for a stable & the other for a lumber room with a loft over both for a corn chamber ... a necessary in the garden with a pigeon house over it
> (National Library of Wales, SA/TERR/535, terrier, Worthenbury rectory, 13th August 1778.)

Until 1858 **wills**, testaments and inventories were proved by episcopal clerks (by a court of civil commission under the Commonwealth). Wills and testaments depict the testator, his family, friends, neighbours, servants, slaves, solicitors and his property (real and movable) and personal circumstances. A testament might extend the testator's will beyond the grave — in the charities and mortifications (hospitals, almshouses, schools) which bear his name, and settlements which encumber an estate for generations.

> Itm. I will and bequeth yt eu[er]more ye iiij p[er]sons as shall happyn to haue ye said houses in pet[er]gat shall haue a house of myn at donnyngton ... yerely to gyf vnto a chauntre preist in ye ministr' which clameth iiijs yerely out of ye new house garth in pet[er]gate vis viijd so yt he and his successors yerely do a masse and a derege wt a p[re]st & hym selfe for ye saules of Eve Cr[ist]ome for ye saule of me John Stokdale.
> (Borthwick Institute of Historical Research, York, probate register 6, folio 186r, John Stokdale of York, merchant, 25th February 1506/7.)

On the death of a testator his house was sealed and friends or neighbours compiled a room by room valuation and **inventory** of contents:

> *Drawing Room*
> Whatnot and Ancient China Ornaments   £2 15s   0d
> Canterbury   10s   0d

Piano Forte	£3	10s	0d
Rosewood inlaid with Pearl small Secretaire	£1	5s	0d
Feather Duster		2s	6d
Gaselier & Fittings	£1	0s	0d
Copper Scuttle		8s	0d

(J. and H. W. Leask, solicitors, Forres, DBA A37/654, A. D. Brands, surgeon, Forres, 1869.)

The **parish vestry**, a meeting of prominent parishioners, convened in the parish church or public house to exercise a benevolent and oligarchic authority over local affairs in England, Ireland and Wales. In Scotland the kirk session from the sixteenth century similarly undertook civil functions (poor relief, charities, education, *et cetera*). Minutes of these parochial parliaments recorded church property (manse, schoolhouse, almshouse, glebe cottage, *et cetera*):

£02=00=00 for the maintenance of Mary Reynill a Lunatick ... [and] ... for the building a partition in John Reynills house for said Lunatick (Public Record Office of Northern Ireland, T679/68, minutes, Ballintoy, County Antrim, 20th April 1747.)

The vestry compiled assessment rolls (listing proprietors, lands and houses), fixed a rate to pay for public and property services, and audited financial accounts of parish officials (churchwarden, surveyor of highways, sexton, beadle, molecatcher, *et cetera*). The parish constable investigated burglaries and housebreakings, visited the haunts of whores and criminals, investigated unruly houses, sought out bastards, and noted the condition of drains, dykes and dungheaps. The office of overseer of the poor appeared in 1572, as an almsgatherer and supervisor of rogues and vagabonds. Workhouses were established from the 1630s onwards and most notably in emulation of the Bristol house (established by act of Parliament in 1696). Small parish workhouses established under a general act of 1722 fell from use with poor law reform in 1834, to be sold or leased and converted into comfortable characterful homes.

The **kirk session**, as moral guardian of the elect in Scotland, dedicated itself to seeking out any breath of scandal and punishing every fall from grace. Domestic privacy was invaded by inquisitorial elders and pruriently priggish neighbours whose findings penetrated to the heart of the Scots home:

scandalous practice has been publickly talked of ... 'twixt Alexr Paterson, Mercht ... and Jean Brodie, Spouse to Wm Duncan ... James Murdoch, Shoemaker ... Depones ... that there is a common Entry to Willm Duncan's House and his, as they lodged then in different Stories of the same house, and that [Brodie] did not return

till about 6 next morning ... Christian Duncan ... Depones ... coming in to Wm Duncan's Room, or Kitchen, she saw ... Alexr Paterson & Jean Brodie sitting together at a window ... [while] Duncan was writing in the shop ... opening the Door of the Kitchen racklessly, she saw Alexr Paterson stand at the Bedside [Brodie's] Gown runkled ... the Bed spread up, and a hollow place in the middle of it.
(Forres Kirk Session, XSFol A2/8, minutes, 17th August 1768.)

Albion House, West Street, Marlow, Buckinghamshire. This vernacular house was refronted in Gothick style and divided to form two dwellings. The use of twelve-pane sashes for the windows, the fancy ironwork and the stiff regularity of the design distinguish the work of an antiquarian-minded romantic architect from that of a medieval master. In this house Shelley completed 'The Revolt of Islam' while Mary Wollstonecraft Shelley prepared her novel 'Frankenstein'. (Photograph: Raymond Lea.)

20. Making a survey

A measured drawing of your old house records in graphic detail for posterity (and for the archives of the local conservation society) the property and its various alterations and improvements. The enlistment of one or two helpers is an advantage, if only to hold the plumbline or one end of the measuring tape.

Much of the equipment required is likely to be available already in your home; other items are readily obtainable from your local stationer and ironmonger. The equipment might include a hardbacked notepad or clipboard; a measuring tape 15 or 30 metres long; a folding rule 2 metres long; a spring-steel tape-measure 2 metres long; a plumbline (a weight attached to a ball of string); pen, pencil, ruler, protractor, eraser, pencil sharpener; a spirit level; a strip of thin lead 25 by 450 mm (for taking impressions of mouldings); a good bright torch (for attics and cellars); binoculars for inaccessible details; a camera for making a permanent photographic record.

With this equipment to hand you may now prepare rough sketch plans, elevations and sections (on squared paper) to be annotated with precise measurements. For a floor plan, measurements are taken horizontally along each wall of each room, and then diagonally across the floor with cross-ties to the door frame, chimney breast, *et cetera*, as a check. It is usual to work clockwise round each room and to record each measurement from point to point either separately or in running fashion with dimension lines and arrows. Your checklist of features to be measured should include: the length across the base of each door and window, the hearth, all fixtures (sink, radiator, bath, copper, *et cetera*), the thickness of the walls (measured at a window or door opening), the width of the staircase and the dimensions of each tread (beware of false assumptions here — the steps may all be of different sizes).

Now turn to the vertical dimension. The height from floor to ceiling of each room is measured. The overall height of the house (except the roofspace) is measured at the stairwell. The difference between these measurements gives the thickness of your floors and ceilings. Changes of floor level are noted at steps up and down.

In the roofspace is a wealth of woodwork — all to be measured. The length and thickness of rafters, posts and purlins are collected with ruler and tape-measure. The angles of the various timbers are measured with a protractor. Large-scale sketches allow you to note the exact forms and dimensions of the pegged and nailed joints which secure the timbers.

Outside the house the length of the walls should be measured along a horizontal plane chosen with the aid of a spirit level (perhaps a course of bricks above the uneven ground surface). Heights (of verge, eaves, chimney stack, ridge, finial, dormer, *et cetera*) can be measured exactly from a ladder. Approximate measurements may be taken by means of a home-made clinometer (a sighting stick fixed against a protractor and made horizontal with a spirit level). The position and size of windows, doors and other features in the walls may be measured from open windows, downwards by plumbline or upwards by folding rule. (Take care when leaning out.)

Interesting details are carefully measured and each is individually drawn in plan and/or section: door (with panelling and frame); window (with mullions, glazing bars and glass lines); floorboard joints (showing position of nails and pegs); roof features (bargeboard, finial, skewput, *et cetera*). In words and symbols added to your sketch plans you may indicate principal building materials (rendered rubble, brick, slate, timber framing, tile hanging, *et cetera*) and wall finishes (paint, plaster, panelling, wallpaper, *et cetera*).

To work up a finished architectural drawing you will require: a drawing board (preferably AO size); tracing paper (or draughting film) and watercolour paper; T-square and adjustable set square (or a draughting machine attached to the drawing board); architectural scale ruler; a range of pencils (4B to 4H); a range of technical pens (0.13 mm to 2.0 mm); springbow compasses (for ink and pencil).

The appropriate scales for architectural drawing are: for plans, elevations and sections, 1:100; for architectural details 1:25, 1:10 (or even larger for the smallest details). A site plan (conventionally drawn with north to the top of the sheet) shows the whole property in relation to neighbouring houses, perhaps at a scale of 1:500.

Floor plans are arranged with the main entrance facing the base of the paper. Doorways are shown at floor level (doorstep indicated); window openings should be included (to permit frames, mullions and glass lines to be represented); stairs are drawn on plan (with arrows and words to indicate 'up' or 'down'). Floor plans should be constructed with the aid of compasses (like a school problem in geometry) using the tied dimensions of your field sketches. A set square cannot be used because an old house is almost certainly not exactly square. To accompany the floor plans you should draw elevations to illustrate the arrangement of windows, doors, drainpipes, dormers and datestones in the front, back and side walls of the house. In addition you should draw one or two sections, showing slices through the building from rooftree to basement, to record floor thickness, ceiling height, foundation depth (a little spadework is required here), and roof-truss configuration.

Plans draughted in pencil are finished in ink. If you have a chance, you might ask your county archivist to show you a selection of architectural drawings (ancient and modern), which will give an impression of the various draughtsmen's conventions in practice as well as giving you ideas for the style and presentation of your own drawings. For your old house you may find that a careful freehand line (rather than a stark ruled line) lends character to the drawing. Hatching and stippling in ink (or Letraset-style transfer) is useful for distinguishing different materials and finishes. Delicate watercolour tints and washes add further refinement. The colours preferred by nineteenth-century draughtsmen are particularly pleasing. These included: pale yellow for masonry in an elevation; grey for slate roofs; blue for windows; brown for woodwork; grey for stone walls, with new or additional work indicated in pink. Your finished drawing should be lettered up ('south elevation', 'first-floor plan', 'section at A-A', *et cetera*). The various rooms should be identified by a single word if possible ('hall', 'kitchen', 'parlour', 'lavatory', 'wc', *et cetera*). Modern architects use a plain stencil for their lettering, but you might prefer to follow earlier convention and add the distinction of your own calligraphy in lettering the plan. A further opportunity for individuation of your drawing is the north point, which should be added in a position where it does not clutter the sheet. Finally, in a box drawn at the bottom right-hand corner of each sheet you should inscribe the name of the surveyor, the address of the property, the date of the survey, the scale of the drawing and other relevant information.

21. Further housework

The expanding discovery of your old house leads into various specialist fields: archaeology, geology, botany — even atomic physics! But do not be dismayed: expert help is readily available. Members of your local vernacular architecture group, local history society and field club (addresses available from the public library) are always pleased to offer friendly advice, or indeed to conduct limited research on your behalf.

Archaeological evidence may carry the history of a house site back ten thousand years as the weekend gardener's spade turns up arrowheads and sharp flint blades (microliths) manufactured by the mesolithic hunters who once camped in the wildwood where now herbaceous borders bloom. In the village of Findhorn in Moray, in 1987, a gardener unearthed from his vegetable patch what seemed to be an old chimney pot from the house. But, knowing that 'the past is ever present', he called in the regional archaeologist (an officer of the local council). The archaeologist immediately recognised the artefact as a cinerary urn of bronze age date. Inside the pot he discovered the cremated remains of a young woman and her newborn infant. The householder generously permitted the local museum to display his precious find, but he returned home uncertain whether to be charmed or chastened by the knowledge that his old house stood on the site of a 4000-year-old cemetery.

Every householder sees every day the various colours and textures of brick, tile, slate and stone in the walls and roof of his home and wonders from time to time where these materials originated. By enlisting the help of a local stonemason or bricklayer — or a geologist friend interested in rocks and fossils — it may be possible to identify the clay pits which supplied the bricks and the quarry which yielded the stones of the house. Building materials shipped from a distance were a mark of wealth and rank, at least until improved means of transport after 1770 brought brick, stone, tile, slate and corrugated iron to all parts of the nation.

The householder might seek the assistance of a local science teacher or an amateur botanist, who, with the aid of a microscope, will be able to identify the different species of wood of which the house is built. Differences in the species (oak, elm, pine, *et cetera*) may indicate successive phases of building or renewal. Timbers can also be precisely dated by expert comparison of patterns of annual growth rings against an established regional pattern. This procedure is known as dendrochronology ('tree dating'). Several universities conduct routine dendrochronological investigations, for example the Palaeoecology Centre, Queen's University, Belfast, charging a set fee for processing a sample of oak and providing a written report. The sample of wood submitted for dating should show at least one hundred annual rings and, preferably, also the last outer sapwood ring (formed in the growing season immediately before the tree was felled). The physical size of the sample is not the limiting factor; indeed quite small pieces of oak may have long ring records — a riven oak plank only 15 cm (6 inches) wide and 1 cm (^{3}/8 inch) thick may preserve as many as two hundred rings, while a massive oak beam 35 cm (14 inches) square may have grown in a mere sixty years. A sample is most easily obtained when timbers are removed during alteration and renovation. Samples from timbers still in position may be obtained by drilling out a core, or by making two parallel cuts halfway through a beam and wedging out the resulting half-slice.

The everyday organic materials from which an old house is constructed (the wood of its beams; the hair which binds its plaster; the straw, dung and twigs of wattle and daub panels) can be dated by the scientific method known as radiocarbon dating. This procedure requires sophisticated laboratory facilities and a sample of about 100 grams of material. Radiocarbon results may be accurate to within a few decades but should always be calibrated against independent criteria such as documentary evidence or carpentry style. Laboratories offering a public service include the Radiocarbon Accelerator Unit of the Research Laboratory for Archaeology and the History of Art, Oxford; the Scottish Universities Research and Reactor Centre, East Kilbride; and the Palaeoecology Centre of Queen's University, Belfast, which specialises in 'high-precision radiocarbon wiggle-matching', guaranteeing very accurate dating.

In discovering your old house you will inevitably accumulate a fat file of notes, drawings, documents and photographs. This file might inspire you to put pen to paper to tell the story of your old house. Writing history requires careful records management. A home computer assists in the organisation of information into a coherent story — a story of past owners, occupants and architectural evolution. The local writers circle (or writer in residence at the county library) would be happy to assist and support your literary endeavours, offering advice, for instance, on typing and presentation. When the story is complete it will deserve pride of place (in a neat folder) on the hall table — an entertaining conversation piece for visiting family and friends. A copy of the history of your old house would be enthusiastically welcomed by the local library. Thus, when the householder is himself a part of history, when his home, barbarously improved or utterly destroyed, is no more than a memory, the written history will remain: a record for later generations and a memorial to the researcher's careful affection for a fragment of his heritage.

22. Further reading

Ayres, J. *The Shell Book of the Home in Britain: Decoration, Design and Construction of Vernacular Interiors, 1500-1850*. Faber, 1981.

Barley, M. W. *Houses and History*. Faber, 1986.

Barrett, H., and Phillips, J. *Suburban Style: the British Home, 1840-1960*. Macdonald, 1987.

Barrett, J., and Iredale, D. *Discovering Old Handwriting*. Shire, 1995.

Brunskill, R. W. *Illustrated Handbook of Vernacular Architecture*. Faber, 1970.

Burnett, John. *A Social History of Housing, 1815-1970*. David & Charles, 1978.

Cunnington, P. *How Old is Your House*. Alphabooks, 1980.

Fleming, J.; Honour, H.; and Pevsner, N. *The Penguin Dictionary of Architecture*. Penguin, 1966.

Hammond, M. *Bricks and Brickmaking*. Shire, second edition 1990.

Harris, R. *Discovering Timber-framed Buildings*. Shire, third edition 1993.

Iredale, D. *Enjoying Archives*. Phillimore, Chichester, second edition 1985.

Mercer, E. *English Vernacular Houses*. HMSO, 1975.

Muthesius, S. *The English Terraced House*. Yale University Press, New Haven, USA, 1982.

Naismith, R. J. *Buildings of the Scottish Countryside*. Gollancz, 1985.

Penoyre, J., and Penoyre, J. *Houses in the Landscape*. Faber, 1978.

Peters, J. E. C. *Discovering Traditional Farm Buildings*. Shire, revised edition 1991.

Powell, C. *Discovering Cottage Architecture*. Shire, reprinted 1996.

Quiney, A. *House and Home*. BBC, 1986.

Reid, R. *The Shell Book of Cottages*. Michael Joseph, 1977.

Saunders, M. *The Historic Home Owner's Companion*. Batsford, 1987.

Shaffrey, P. and M. *Buildings of the Irish Countryside*. O'Brien, Dublin, 1985.

Smith, P. *Houses of the Welsh Countryside*. HMSO, second edition 1988.

West, J. *Village Records*. Macmillan, 1962.

West, T. W. *Discovering English Architecture*. Shire, 1979.

West, T. W. *Discovering Scottish Architecture*. Shire, 1985.

Wiliam, E. *Home Made Homes. Dwellings of the Rural Poor in Wales*. National Museum of Wales, 1988.

23. Useful addresses

The principal archive-holding institutions of Britain are listed in the current editions of *Record Repositories in Great Britain* (Her Majesty's Stationery Office for the Royal Commission on Historical Manuscripts) and *British Archives* by J. Foster and J. Sheppard (Macmillan). *Whitaker's Almanack* contains addresses for government departments, royal commissions, national societies and institutions. *The Directory of British Associations* (periodically updated) contains details by title and subject of local and national organisations, such as the Vernacular Architecture Group. The local reference librarian will be able to put the researcher in touch with local contacts for national organisations such as the Georgian Group, Victorian Society, Thirties Society, Society of Architectural Historians. The names and addresses of fellow historians and local field clubs will be known to the local studies librarian. Other useful addresses — of solicitors, architects, estate factors, landowners, church officials, company secretaries, *et cetera* — are also available in the library.

Seatown of Lossiemouth, Moray, Grampian. The fisher folk of the outport of the burgh of Elgin originally lived at the mouth of the river Lossie. In 1784 the land on which their houses stood was required for redevelopment. The houses were demolished and the families removed to new houses built at the burgh's expense a short distance up river at Seatown. This early 'council housing' scheme is comprehensively documented in the burgh archives. As in most fisher villages the rows of houses in Seatown stood gable-end to the shore. In the spaces between the rows the fishermen spread their nets and erected sheds, huts, net stores and even a village shop. These outhouses, with some modest remodelling, make cosy homes. (Photograph: John Barrett.)

Glossary

Abutments: in carpentry scarf joints, the ends of halved timbers — perhaps with tongue-and-groove elaborations: **bridled** or **bladed** to limit lateral or vertical movement.

Aisle: part of a house separated from the main part by a row of posts.

Apron: panel below a window sill.

Architrave: a moulding, generally around a door or window.

Arts and Crafts: late nineteenth-century decorative style emphasising hand craftsmanship.

Ashlar: smooth, square-hewn stone used to face rubble or bricks.

Assize (eyre): a national court sitting locally.

Axial stack: house built around a central chimney stack.

Baluster: a stumpy pillar supporting a handrail.

Bargain and sale: type of title deed.

Bargeboard: decorative board on a gable.

Baronial: Scottish castellated style.

Bastle: northern defensible house.

Bay: a single structural unit; also a projecting window.

Blue book: a government publication.

Bolection moulding: decorative strip covering a joint.

Bond: the pattern of bricks in a wall.

Brace: diagonal reinforcement.

Bressumer: a beam spanning an opening.

But-and-ben: two-roomed highland house.

Calendar: an archival catalogue.

Capitular records: cathedral archives.

Casement: side-hung hinged window.

Catslide: sloping roof extended downwards to cover an extension.

Cess: assessment for local tax.

Cestui que use: legal beneficiary.

Chancery: a department and court of government.

Chantry: an endowment for a priest singing masses for the soul.

Chartulary: a collection of charters, deeds, *et cetera*.

Close Roll: a national record of documents issued.

Clunch: a soft chalk building stone.

Cob: mud and straw walling material.

Cobble: a large water-rounded stone.

Coffering: decorative division into rectangular panels.

Collar: crossbeam linking opposite rafters.

Commissary: Scottish court exercising jurisdiction over testaments.

Common Pleas: national court of law.

Common recovery: a title deed created by collusive court action.

Conveyance: transfer of property.

Copyhold: type of manorial tenure.

Corbelling: projecting masonry courses.

Cottage orné: decoratively rustic cottage.

Crenellation: battlemented parapet.

Crocket: a Gothic pinnacle.

Crosspassage: passage crossing house from back to front.

Crosswing: wing built at right angle to hall.

Crown plate: longitudinal timber beam resting on head of crown post.

Crown post: vertical timber rising from tiebeam.

Crowstep: gable formed like a flight of steps.

Crucks: curved paired timbers forming structural frame.

Cusping: pointed elements in Gothic tracery.

Customary tenure: possession according to the tradition and custom of the manor.

Deal: sawn softwood planking.

Dean of Guild: Scottish building control authority.

Deed: document concerning property transaction; in Scotland a formal authenticated document.

Deed poll: a deed cut square at the head — not an indenture.

Demesne: manorial home farm.

Demise: conveyance of property by will or lease.

Dendrochronology: dating of timbers from pattern of annual growth rings.

Diaper: pattern of lozenges or squares.

Diocese: territory of a bishop.

Dogleg stair: staircase with 180 degree turn and no central well.

Dormer: window sprouting from a sloping roof.

Dorse: back of a document on which endorsements are written.

Dragon beam: a diagonal beam in hipped roofs and jetties.

Dripstone: projecting masonry course above a window or door.

Drystone: masonry without mortar.

Dutch (or Flemish) gable: curved, perhaps pedimented, end wall.

Ejectment: document dispossessing by legal process.

Elevation: a façade; a drawing of a façade.

Enclosure: legal process for clearing, dividing, fencing and reallocating common lands.

Entablature: in classical architecture, the composite term for architrave, frieze and cornice.

Entail: legal settlement limiting descent of property.

Equity: natural justice (rather than common or statute law).

Excambion: an exchange of property.

Exchequer: fiscal court and department of government.

Fanlight: window over a door.

Fee simple: the most complete form of property ownership (freehold).

Feu, fee: land held from a feudal lord (superior).

Fine: title deed based on a feigned action at law.

Fireback: cast iron plate at the back of a fireplace.

Framing: pattern outlined by external structural timbers.

Fresco: painting executed on wet plaster.

Gable: a triangular end wall.

Girding beam: horizontal beam supporting ends of upper-floor joists.

Glebe: land forming part of a clergyman's benefice.

Gothick: medieval style revived in later architecture.

Hall: all-purpose room of a medieval house.

Halving: in carpentry, a joint of mirror-image cutaways.

Harling: external wall coating of lime and gravel.

Hatchment: coat of arms, heraldic achievement.

Header: a brick laid so that its head appears in the face of a wall.

Hearth tax: a tax on fireplaces.

Hipped roof: roof with sloping ends and sides.

Hundred rolls: county surveys of Crown rights and revenues.

Incumbered estate: property tied down by financial or legal obligations.

Indenture: document written twice on a single leaf and the duplicates divided by an irregular cut.

Inglenook: recess with seat beside fireplace.

Inquisition post mortem: feudal inquiry into deceased person's property.

Inventory: list of possessions for probate.

Jamb: side post of doorway.

Jetty: overhanging upper storey.

Joist: timber supporting floorboards.

Keystone: central tapering stone in an arch.

King post: roof timber rising from collar or tiebeam to ridge.

King's Bench: a national court of law.

Label mould: moulded dripstone.

Lacing course: course of brick or squared masonry reinforcing a rubble wall.

Laithe house: northern house with barn/byre attached.

Lancet: narrow aperture with pointed head.

Lap joint: carpentry joint where one timber fits into a cutaway on another.

Lavatory: place for washing.

Lease: document granting possession for a specified term; with **release**, a deed of title.

Ledger: financial account book.

Letter book: a book of copy correspondence.

Liege: a person subject to a feudal superior.

Linenfold: carved pattern resembling folded cloth.

Link snuffer: fixture for extinguishing flaming torches.

Lintel: horizontal beam bridging window, door, *et cetera*.

Longhouse: house with lower-end stalling for cattle.

Louvre: slatted opening.

Lying pane: glazing style of horizontal oblong panes.

Manor: feudal administrative and territorial unit.

Mansard: roof of which each face has two slopes.

Marriage lintel: lintel carved with initials of spouses and date of marriage.

Mason mark: device carved on a stone identifying the mason responsible.

Mathematical tile: tile resembling brick.

Megalith: 'big stone', especially prehistoric; often reused in later buildings.

Merlon: solid part of battlemented parapet.

Messuage: in title deeds, a house with pertinents.

Misbedding: stone laid unconformably.

Modern movement: rectilinear twentieth-century style (**moderne**).

Mortgage: document securing a loan against property.

Mortice and tenon: carpentry joint with protruding male tenon fitting into a female mortice slot.

Mud and stud: walling of light framing and daub.

Mullion: vertical post dividing a window opening.

Muniments: collection of documents.

Newel: principal post of a staircase.

Nogging: brick infill of timber frame.

Notary public: legal official authorised to record deeds.

Ogee: a double-curved arch.

Oriel: an upstairs projecting window.

Outshut: rear extension to a house.

Oversailing brickwork: overhanging or projecting courses.

Palladian: the neo-classical style of Andrea Palladio (1508-80).

Pantile: S-section clay roofing tile.

Parchment: sheepskin writing surface.

Pargeting: decorative plasterwork.

Patent: an official document issued open for all to see.

Pattern book: an exemplar of architectural or decorative style.

Pebbledash: exterior wall coating of mortar with pebbles.

Pediment: gable above a classical portico.

Pend: a tunnel-like alleyway.

Penthouse: building (usually a shed or annexe) with sloping roof; also an attic apartment

Piazza: a covered colonnaded walkway.

Piend: edge or angle formed at the meeting of two surfaces

Pilaster: decorative column slightly projecting from a wall.

Pile: a building **single pile** when one room deep; **double pile** when two rooms deep.

Pisé: a rammed-earth walling material.

Placeman: holder of an office of profit under the Crown.

Plank and muntin: a style of partitioning of vertical timbers.

Pointing: mortar finishing of masonry joints.

Polite: urbane architectural style.

Portico: a classical entranceway.

Post and truss (box frame): timber framing comprising wall posts, wall frames and roof trusses — not cruck construction.

Prerogative court: archbishop's probate court.

Presbytery: a court in the Church of Scotland.

Protocol book: a local register of deeds.

Purlin: longitudinal roof timber.
Puttstone: stone at base of skew.
Quatrefoil: four-leaf decoration.
Quoin: dressed corner stones.
Rafter: roof timber from wallhead to roof.
Rainwater head: hopper at top of drainpipe.
Range: one-piece metal solid-fuel kitchen stove.
Regality: feudal administrative and territorial unit.
Relieving arch: arch to relieve loading on a lintel.
Remainder: residual interest in an estate.
Rendering: weatherproof skin for exterior wall.
Ridge: the longitudinal timber at the roof apex.
Roughcast: exterior wall coating of cement mixed with gravel.
Rubbed brick: shaped brick.
Rubble: unshaped stone.
Sarking: boarding on rafters.
Sash window: sliding window frame.
Sasine: a document witnessing the change of feudal possession of property.
Scarf: carpentry joint for joining timbers longitudinally.
Screens passage: passage between hall and service end.
Sequestration: confiscation of property.
Service of heirs: document concerning succession to property.
Session, Court of: Scottish central civil and criminal court.
Sessional paper: a parliamentary record.
Sessions, Court of Great: Welsh court of law.
Settlement: legal arrangement, for example between spouses.
Skew: the slope of a gable wall from ridge to **skewput**.
Smoke bay: narrow bay for hearth.
Smoke hood: timber-framed hood above hearth.
Soffit: undersurface, for example of an arch.
Solar: private room in a medieval house.
Spandrel: triangular space between brace, post and beam.
Speculum: ecclesiastical property survey.
Stake and rice: walling of light framing and daub.
State paper: government document particularly on home affairs.
Statesman: Cumbrian yeoman.
Statutory list: national list of buildings of special architectural or historical interest; listed buildings.
Stent: assessment for local tax.
Stretcher: brick laid so that its side appears in the face of a wall.
String course: projecting horizontal course along an exterior wall.
Strut: roof timber connecting rafter to collar or king post.
Stucco: plaster or cement coating for exterior wall.
Stud: a non-structural vertical timber.
Superior: feudal overlord.
Survey: a word picture of a property.

Swag: ornamental festoon.
Sway: a pliable twig or rod used in thatching or for wattle.
Synod: a church court.
Tack: Scottish form of lease.
Tenement: a property holding; also multi-storeyed flatted housing.
Terrace: three or more houses linked in a row.
Terracotta: unglazed earthenware.
Terrier: an ecclesiastical property survey.
Testament: a bequest of possessions (originally not real estate).
Testator: a person making a will or testament.
Throughstone: stone running through the thickness of a wall.
Tiebeam: transverse timber linking the feet of paired rafters.
Tithe: a church tax (a tenth part).
Torching: pointing for stone roof.
Tracery: ornamental openwork in Gothic windows.
Transom: horizontal beam dividing a window opening.
Trenail: a wooden peg securing a carpentry joint.
Turnpike stair: spiral stair.
Turnpike trust: administration for a toll road.
Tŷ hir: longhouse (Welsh).
Undercroft: room below a first-floor hall.
Use: a beneficiary interest in a property.
Venetian window: tripartite window with arched central element.
Vernacular: traditional native style.
Vestry: parochial governing committee.
Voucher: financial document; also a legal guarantor.
Voussoir: wedge-shaped stone in an arch.
Wainscot: wooden lining for interior walls.
Wallplate: longitudinal timber along wallhead
Warrantor: a legal guarantor.
Wattle and daub: walling of woven laths plastered with mud or dung.
Wealden house: the hall with crosswings of Kent and Sussex.
Weatherboarding: wall cladding of horizontal planks.
Witchert: earth, clunch and clay walling material.
Yeoman: type of English freeholder.
Yorkshire sash: horizontally sliding window.

Index

Page numbers in italic refer to ill‘ustrations.

Accounts (finance) 66, 79, 80, 83, 95, 97
Aisle 9
Almshouse 53, 86, 90, 97
Archaeology 102
Architects 83-4
Art Déco 51
Art Nouveau 51
Arts and Crafts 59, 86
Ashlar *16*, 17
Auctioneer 84-5
Axial stack *13*, 13-14
Back-to-back 15, 55
Bankruptcy 84, 94
Bargain and sale 75
Bargeboard 41, 58
Baronial 7
Bastle 9
Bay 24, *26*, 96
Bond *20*, 23
Botany 102
Box frame *26*, 26-7, 29
Brick *8*, *18*, 20, 20-3, 21, 22, 45-6, *46*, 49, 58, 59
Bridging beam 43, *44*
Building regulation 22, 32, 59, 65, 89, 89-90
Bungalow 58, *59*, *60*
But-and-ben 12
Byre *36*, 56-7
Cellar 22, *28*, 54
Central heating 8, 47, 88
Chancery 92
Chartulary 73-4
Chimney *8*, *10*, 12, 13, *13*, *15*, *16*, 29, 33, 45-6, *46*, *57*, 58, *86*, *94*
Church 8
Church archive 95-8
Cladding 31-3
Classicism *7*, *16*, 22, 48, *48*, 58
Clay lump 18-19
Close studding *12*, 26-7, *27*, *29*, *57*
Cob 18-19, *19*
Cobble 17-18, *18*
Collar *34*, 35
Common recovery 73
Contract 83-4, 90
Copyhold 76
Cottage orné 58, *59*
Council house 59, 60, 90
Court record 82, 87, 89, 93-4, 95
Crescent 22, 53
Crofting *15*, 93
Crosspassage 10, *11*, 14, 36
Crosswing 9-10
Crown post *34*, 35
Crowstep 23, 41, *41*, *42*, 62
Cruck 24, *26*, *26*, 81
Customary tenure 76
Datestone *21*, *36*, *38*, *41*, *42*, *50*, 58, 62
Daub *26*, 31, *31*, 45, 89
Dendrochronology *11*, 102-3

Directory 63
Door, *7*, *8*, *10*, *16*, 22, *38*, 47-8, *48*, *57*, 58
Double end 9-10, *11*
Double front 15
Double pile 15, 39, *40*, 59
Dragon post 29, *30*
Draughting 101
Dutch gable *8*, *40*, *41*, 59
Electricity 8, 52
Enclosure *21*, 57, 82, 87-8, 94
Entail 75-6
Ephemera 79, 83
Estate 55-6, 80-2, 95
Estate agent 84-5
Exchequer 92
Fee simple 71
Feoffment 71-2, 74, 75
Fine 72-3
Fireback 45
Fire regulation 22, 65
First-floor hall 9, *10*, 66
Flint 18
Floor 43, 89
Forestair *66*, 89
Framing patterns 26-7, *27*, 28
Fresco 44
Gablet *12*, 39, 45
Gas 52, 97
Gazetteer 62
Geology 102
Girding beam 43
Glass 48-9, *49*, 51, *51*, 62, 90
Gothic/Gothick 58, *91*, *98*
Government records 92-4
Grate 46-7
Great rebuilding 6, 42
Guidebook 61-2
Guttering 41
Hall 9-10, *11*, *12*, *33*, *94*
Harling 33, *42*, 66
Hearth 9, 10, 11, 12, 13, *13*, 14, *37*, 45-7
Highland 6-7
Hip 6, *12*, *15*, 39-40, *40*, 59
Historical Monuments Commissions 63, 65-6, 83
Illustration 3, 62, 67-8
Infilling 31, *31*
Inglenook 45, *45*
Insurance 83
Interviewing 3, 5
Inventory 81, 96-7
Ironwork 41, 58, *91*, *98*
Jetty 10, *11*, 29, *29*, *30*, *32*, *33*, *94*
Joint 24, *24*, 25, 43, *44*
Joist *16*, 29, *29*, 30, 43, *44*
King post *34*, 35
Kirk session 95, 97-8
Laithe 57
Lawyers 85
Lease 75, 80, 81
Licensing *32*, 87

Linenfold 43, *44*
Listed building 4, *28*, *38*, 88
Literature 64
Local government 89-91
Longhouse 9, *36*, 56
Lowland 6-7
Manor 76, 78, 82
Mansard 40, *40*
Map 61, 67, 68-70, 71, 82
Marriage lintel *50*, 58, 62
Memoirs 79
Modern movement 52, 60, *60*
Mortgage 71, 81
Moulding 35, 43, 46, 48, *49*, 58
Mud and stud 19
Names *32*, *33*, 42, 77-8, 88
Newspaper 63-4
Nogging 31, *31*, 57
Ordnance Survey 69-70
Oriel 48
Oven *46*, 47, *57*, 58
Panelling 43-4, *44*
Pantile *10*, 39, *40*, 59
Pargeting 32-3, *33*
Parish 95, 97-8
Parliament 65
Pattern book *56*, 61
Pebbledash 57
Penthouse *57*, 58, *94*
Perambulation 61
Petition 89
Pevsner, N. 63
Photograph 3, 68, 83, 84
Piazza *42*, 53
Pisé 19
Plan 3, *60*, 61, 66, 70, 71, 81, 82, 83-4, 85, 89-90, 100-1
Plank and muntin 43
Planning *32*, 53, 55-6, 89-90
Plaster 32-3, *33*, 44-5, 89, 91
Polite 6, 7, 7, 16, 86
Porch 13, *27*, *36*, 57, 57
Postcard 68
Privy Council 92-3
Protocol book 73
Pub *30*, *32*, 87
Purlin *26*, *34*, 35-6
Quarter sessions 87-8
Queen post *34*
Radiocarbon 102
Rafter *26*, 35
Range *46*, 47
Release 75
Rendering 32-3
Rental 80-1
Roof *16*, *28*, 29, *33*, *34*, 35-41, *37*, *40*, *42*, 58, 99-100
Rubble 4, *15*, 17, *37*, 57, *57*, 58
Sale 64, 82, 84-5
Sanitation *11*, 29, 51-2, 52, 81, 91, 96, 97

Schoolhouse 85-6, *90*, *97*
Seisin 71, 72, 74, 75
Semi-detached 55-6, *57*, *60*
Side 81
Single end 9, *12*, *33*, *94*
Single front 15
Single pile 15, 29
Skew 41, *41*
Slate 4, *28*, 38-9
Smoke bay *44*, 45
Smoke hood 45, 90
Solar 9, *10*, *11*, *94*
Specification 63-4, 83, 90
Square 53, 55
Stair 10, 12, 13, 14, *29*, *36*, 47, *66*, 72, 89
Stake and rice 19, 85
State paper 92-3
Stone 4, 17-18, *36*, *37*, 37-9, *38*, *42*, *49*, 55, 91, 102
Stucco 33, 58, *91*
Suburbia *52*, 58, 59-60, *60*
Survey 64, 81-2, 91, 92, 95-6
Surveying 4, 5, 99-101
Taxation 21, 87, 91, 92, 93, 97
Terrace *38*, 53, *54*, 55, 55, *56*, 58, 86
Terracotta 39, *39*, 40-1, *46*, 59, 96
Thatch *29*, *33*, 36-7, *36*, *37*, 59, *94*
Tiebeam *24*, 26
Tile *29*, 31-2, *33*, 37-8, *39*, *39*, *42*, 59
Timber framing *11*, *12*, 23-4, 26-7, *26*, *29*, 43, *44*, *94*
Tithe 70
Title deed *32*, *50*, 71-6, 80, 87, *88*, 90, 92
Tollhouse 8, *59*, 85
Truss *34*, 35-6
Trust 74-5
Undercroft 9, *10*
Use 74-5
Vernacular 6, *57*, 58, 61, 63
Vernacular revival 59, *60*, 86
Vestry 97
Victoria County Histories 62-3
Visitation 95-6
Wattle *26*, 31, *31*
Wealden 9-10, *11*, 53
Weatherboard 31, *32*, *94*
Wichert 19
Will 71, 74, 95, 96-7
Window 4, *8*, *10*, *16*, *28*, *38*, *42*, 48-9, *49*, *50*, 51, *51*, *52*, 54, 55, 58, 86, *98*
Workhouse 90, 97
Writing 103